SACRED MEDICINE
Exploring The Psychedelic Hero's Journey

A Transformative Path of Self-Discovery and Spiritual Awakening through Sacred Medicine Ceremonies and Shamanic Rituals

by 1Drea Pennington Wasio, M.D., C.Ac.
Formerly known as Andrea Pennington
with Gregg Westwood & Irina Vlada

Featuring stories by:

Gregg Westwood — Irina Vlada

Aimee Callahan, PhD — Niki Charlie

Kate Church — Jamie Church

Cindy Coats — Julia Squared

1Drea Pennington Wasio, MD

Kathy Hill — Myrthe de Jongh

Valencia Khoza — Chen Lizra

John Jacob Mubarak — Sandra Dee Nicholson

KaRen Marie Quiles — Jeannine Sanderson

Jill Stocker, DO — Andi Wagner

MAKE YOUR MARK GLOBAL

MAKE YOUR MARK GLOBAL PUBLISHING, LTD

USA & Monaco

Lead Editor: Lynette Stewart
Proofread by Samantha Lord
Book cover design: Andrea Danon & Stefan Komljenović of Art Biro Network
www.artbiro.ba

Library of Congress Cataloging-in-Publication Data
Library of Congress Control Number: 2023936082
Sacred Medicine
Publisher: Make Your Mark Global, LTD
Ft. Myers, Florida
p315
Trade Paperback ISBN 979-8-9881368-1-1
Ebook ISBN 979-8-9881368-0-4

Subjects: Psychology

Summary: In *Sacred Medicine* Dr. 1Drea Pennington, formerly known as Andrea Pennington, presents a collection of 25 personal stories and cautionary tales. This book illuminates the potential benefits and risks of using powerful psychedelic tools for personal growth and healing. The authors take readers on a Hero's Journey through various psychedelic plants, fungi, and shamanic rituals and spiritual traditions that have been used for centuries for healing, growth, and transformation.

MAKE YOUR MARK GLOBAL PUBLISHING, LTD
USA

For information on bulk purchase orders of this book or to book Dr. 1Drea to speak at your event or on your program, call +33 06 12 74 77 09 or send an email to Booking@AndreaPennington.com

Also Compiled or Co-authored by Daess 1Drea Pennington Wasio, MD

The Top 10 Traits of Highly Resilient People

Holistic Healing

Manifesting Love

Magic and Miracles

Life After Trauma

Time to Rise

Turning Points / Vendepunkter

Heart to Heart: The Path to Wellness

Resilience Through Yoga and Meditation

Dedication

To my dear friend Celena, you were my first guide into sacred lands and spiritual vistas.
Because of you, my life is full of the presence of angels.
You are deeply appreciated and terribly missed.

To my colleague and favorite cheerleader, Dr. T., your loving support and belief in me helped me to embrace all of my gifts. You will be remembered forever.

To you, dear reader, may the wisdom and experiences shared within these pages serve as a beacon of light, guiding you on your path and reminding you that you are not alone in your quest for deeper understanding and connection.

May we all continue to explore the mysteries of the universe and the infinite possibilities that lie within us.

Preface

So, you've heard the call to explore psychedelics and shamanism. You're in good company! As we see in a barrage of documentaries, daytime television interviews, podcasts, salacious stories on magazine stands, and hyped-up newspaper headlines, psychedelics are proving to be the next hot thing to experiment with, invest in, and brag about.

From individual sessions of Psychedelic Assisted Therapy and personal development retreats with sacred plant medicines, to microdosing psychedelic substances and jetting off to foreign lands for immersive experiences with shamans in the jungle, there are so many ways to experience psychedelics these days. Research shows that psychedelics have the potential to help veterans recover from PTSD, support bereaved parents in processing the grief of losing a child, and facilitate healing of racial trauma in marginalized individuals. Silicon Valley techies swear by the effects of increased creativity and focus with small and large doses of LSD or psilocybin mushrooms, and even moms across America affirm that taking sub-hallucinatory doses of psychedelics makes them happier, more stable mothers. There are many benefits that continue to impress even the most skeptical science-minded folks.

It sounds appealing to hear that a visit to a shaman or a visionary psychedelic trip down the rabbit hole has the potential to help you kick a longstanding addiction in one session, heal hidden trauma, stimulate an ego death, and lead you to be reborn as your Authentic Self. But many ask, is it worth the risk of potential legal trouble, the steep financial cost, and intense physiological purge?

The reports of abuse by shady shamans and 'bad trips' abound, which makes one pause to reconsider whether a getting a glimpse of what lies behind the veil of this known reality is worth it.

Despite questions of safety and legality, people are turning up in droves to retreat centers, ordering psychedelic compounds on the dark web, and learning to grow their own mushrooms. Patients facing terminal diagnoses are petitioning the government for special access to psychedelic treatments to calm their anxiety and prepare for the inevitable. It's as if there is a deep call to explore the depths of the unconscious and find healing in new lands.

The call to sit with a shaman or partake in a psychedelic journey is very much like the Call to Adventure as described by Joseph Campbell in the Hero's Journey, as outlined in his book *The Hero with a Thousand Faces*. In fact, many aspects of shamanic ceremonies and psychedelic trips are aligned with most steps of the Hero's Journey, which is what inspired me to organize the stories in this book following that framework.

I was first introduced to the Hero's Journey while studying film and theatre at university almost 30 years ago. I learned that Joseph Campbell, an American writer and lecturer, studied myths, tales and stories from cultures around the world. His research showed that across time and across cultures, humans tell the same types of stories, with a similar structure, and even a recurring cast of characters that show up in our myths, fables, and movies consistently. The Hero's Journey is a story archetype that touches people because it mirrors the trials and tribulations of our own lives. This journey structure resonates so deeply with the human psyche that it is the #1 reason that films and books become bestsellers. It even explains why we get so moved by great films — even the kiddie movies!

The concept of the Hero's Journey has been an enduring and powerful narrative archetype throughout human history which speaks to our deep-seated desire for transformation, adventure, and self-discovery. At the same time, the use of psychedelics and participation in shamanic ceremonies have been a part of many cultures for thousands of years, providing individuals with the opportunity to explore altered states of consciousness and potentially experience profound shifts in their worldview and sense of self. What if the Hero's Journey wasn't just a metaphorical construct, but an actual experience that we could undergo in our own lives? What if it was similar to taking psychedelics and entering shamanic ceremonies, full of possibility as well as potential perils?

Many people who have taken psychedelics describe their experiences as a profound personal journey that mirrors the structure of the Hero's Journey. At the beginning of the journey, the hero is often called to adventure by an inner or outer force. Similarly, people who take psychedelics often feel a calling to explore their consciousness and gain new insights into themselves and the world around them.

As the hero embarks on their journey, they encounter various obstacles and challenges that test their resolve and force them to confront their deepest fears and weaknesses. Similarly, people who take psychedelics often experience intense and sometimes difficult emotions and sensations that challenge their sense of self and push them to confront their inner demons.

As the hero overcomes these challenges, they gain new knowledge, wisdom, and strength, and ultimately reach a state of enlightenment or self-realization. Similarly, people who take psychedelics may emerge from the experience transformed, and often report gaining profound insights and perspectives on themselves and the world around them, which can lead to a greater sense of meaning and purpose in their lives.

And just as the hero may return home to share their newfound wisdom with their community, a person who has undergone a psychedelic experience may feel compelled to share their insights with others or to use their recently discovered understanding to create positive change in their life and the world around them.

Ultimately, the Hero's Journey is about transformation and growth, and people who take psychedelics or sit with shamans often describe their experiences as transformative and life-changing. However, it's worth noting that the journey doesn't end with the experience itself; like the hero, people who take psychedelics must integrate their insights and newfound knowledge into their everyday lives in order to truly embody the transformation that they've undergone.

In *Sacred Medicine*, we will explore the similarities between the Hero's Journey and the use of psychedelics and shamanic ceremonies. Both involve a journey of self-discovery with potential for great rewards, leading to profound changes in our perception of ourselves and the world around us. But they are also ripe with potential perils. Just as the hero must face trials and tribulations on their quest for transformation, taking psychedelics and entering shamanic ceremonies can bring us face to face with our deepest fears and anxieties, leading to potentially challenging and traumatic experiences, including the possibility of psychological distress and destabilization. It is clear that those who embark on a psychedelic journey or participate in a shamanic ceremony will certainly confront their own fears, limitations, and shadow selves, just as a Hero does in an epic tale.

Drawing upon the wisdom of ancient traditions combined with personal anecdotes and modern scientific research, we offer a comprehensive exploration of the Hero's Journey as it relates to psychedelic and shamanic experiences. Together we will delve into the ways in which these experiences can help us to better understand our purpose and meaning in life. We will also explore the potential pitfalls and dangers associated with these journeys, and provide insight for those who are considering exploring these realms for themselves.

Finally, this book is an invitation to explore the Hero's Journey in a new and profound way, by venturing into the world of psychedelics and shamanic ceremonies. It is a call to embrace the full spectrum of human experience, with all its possibilities and perils, and to emerge on the other side as a more fully realized and integrated individual. Whether you are a seasoned traveler on the path of self-discovery or a curious newcomer, this book offers valuable insights and guidance for navigating the transformative journey that lies ahead.

Of course, not everyone who takes psychedelics will experience a Hero's Journey in this way, and there can be risks and challenges involved in taking these substances. It's important to approach these experiences with caution and respect, and to seek guidance from experienced practitioners or professionals along the way.

CONTENT WARNING:

The book you are about to read contains accounts of personal experiences that touch upon sensitive and potentially triggering subjects. The authors bravely share their stories, which may include references to trauma, such as attempted murder, suicidal ideation, and a history of sexual and physical abuse.

While the purpose of this book is to explore the transformative power of sacred plant medicine and its potential for healing and growth, we acknowledge that these topics can evoke strong emotional responses in readers. We believe it is important to provide a space for open and honest storytelling, but we also recognize the potential impact it may have on individuals who have experienced similar traumas.

We encourage readers to approach this book with self-care and to be mindful of their own emotional well-being. If you find that the content becomes overwhelming, we recommend taking breaks or seeking support from trusted friends, family, or mental health professionals.

Remember, the stories within these pages reflect the individual experiences of the authors, and while they can provide valuable insights and perspectives, they may not necessarily apply to everyone's journey or experiences.

By choosing to read this book, you acknowledge and accept the presence of potentially triggering content. We hope that the stories shared within will offer inspiration, healing, and a deeper understanding of the human spirit.

Please proceed with self-care and compassion for yourself and others as we embark on this exploration of the psychedelic hero's journey through sacred medicine ceremonies and shamanic rituals.

Contents

Introduction

My heroic journey into the world of shamanic ceremony and psychedelic healing started out in an ordinary world of sadness and gloom. I lived with depressive thoughts for the first three decades of my life. I have a deep knowing of what it feels like to not want to be alive anymore. As a kid I fantasized about what a relief death would bring.

Over the course of my early life, I tried many things to alleviate my dark moods and sadness, with little to no success. Antidepressants and talk therapy didn't relieve my depression much at all. Creative arts helped some. But deep inside I didn't feel happiness was possible for me.

As I've shared some of my personal story, you'll see that in the last decade psychedelic medicines and shamanic ceremonies have accelerated and deepened the healing of my childhood trauma, connected me to my essential Self, and expanded my ability to fully embody my life on earth.

My motivation to publicly disclose my psychedelic use is for harm reduction, education, and to potentially save lives. I've lost two dear friends to suicide in the last few years. And I believe that Psychedelic Assisted Therapy could have saved their lives. This is why I've recently broken my silence about attending sacred plant medicine ceremonies with ayahuasca and magic mushrooms.

And this is also why I completed a fellowship and received certification in Psychedelic Assisted Therapy to provide Ketamine sessions, which are legal in the USA, as well as psilocybin and MDMA when they are legalized. This is why I help facilitate psilocybin mushroom ceremonies in countries where they are legal, with an experienced team of facilitators and medicine men and women.

As an integrative physician, acupuncturist, and meditation teacher with specialty training in trauma recovery, addiction medicine and eating disorder recovery, my aim is to help people find the right modalities to activate your innate vitality code to boost resilience, nurture real self-love, and find confidence in your own inner healing capacity. For over 20 years, I've offered healing and education in my wellness practice, in the media, on stages and around the world in workshops and retreats. In these two decades of medical practice I have seen the immense benefit of integrating complementary modalities that address the physical, emotional, spiritual, relational, and environmental aspects life. We are holistic beings, and we require holistic healing.

Even when we are addressing physical health conditions, we must conduct a 360-degree analysis of a person's makeup and dive deep into the psyche to root out the source of dis-ease — including the limiting beliefs, unhealed wounds, and disconnection from one's true identity. I believe this integrative, holistic approach that weaves together depth psychology, neuroscience, shamanic ceremony, and Psychedelic Assisted Therapy can do wonders for addressing unmet medical and mental health needs, especially for marginalized people such as LGBTQIA+ queer, and BIPOC, Black Indigenous People of Color, also known as People of the Global Majority[1].

We are all on a Hero's Journey, it's a journey of self-discovery, tests and trials, death and ultimately transformation. Just being born is a heroic journey for both mother and baby. As a child dies to its infantile personality to become an adult, it moves from dependency to sovereignty and independence. As we grow and evolve, we will also be inspired to share what we learn with others to help them on their journey.

True healing and transformation isn't a one-time event. It unfolds over many years and takes work for most of us. And even with the miraculous support of psychedelics, healing requires that we un-learn old ways of behaving, thinking, and emoting. Integrating what we see and understand from our shamanic and psychedelic journeys is just as important as taking the substance.

Not a cure-all, but better than standard treatments

As I've transformed with the support of sacred medicines and shamanic ceremonies, I see the tremendous benefit of highlighting the importance of educated, informed use of these powerful allies. Psychedelics are certainly not a cure-all, but in my experience, they can be far more potent than standard medical treatment and talk therapy in many instances.

---

[1] People of the Global Majority refers to people who are Black, Asian, Brown, dual-heritage, indigenous to the global south, and or have been racialized as 'ethnic minorities'.

It's well-known that existing medications and psychotherapy for depression, substance use disorder, anxiety, and PTSD are not 100% effective in all cases. And neither are psychedelics.

The clinical studies on MDMA, psilocybin, ketamine, ayahuasca, ibogaine, and LSD happening today and over the last three decades reveal the possibility of treatments that lead to lasting results, as well as often immediate relief of suicidal thoughts. But psychedelic therapies are not for everyone. However, for those with severe PTSD, treatment resistant depression and existential angst, these medicines may offer partial relief and stabilization. It is especially crucial that the right medicine is chosen and is that it is delivered by a competent, compassionate caregiver, in the right setting, with the proper dosage, with clear intentions and post-dosing integration.

Despite the origins of sacred ceremonies with plant, animal and fungal medicine in South America, Africa and Asia, this psychedelic space has been dominated by White people in the past 150 years. The so-called whitewashing of the psychedelic renaissance exists for a multitude of reasons, from lack of access to concerns of legality, particularly with the over-representation of black and brown inmates from drug-related offenses, to the limitation in the racial makeup of research subjects and scholars.

That said, living with covert and blatant racial traumas and microaggressions puts Black and Brown people at risk for harm when entering a psychedelic assisted therapy session or shamanic ceremony. Many researchers and clinicians including Sara Reed and Monnica Williams have highlighted the risk of harm to Black and Brown people in psychedelic assisted therapy settings with facilitators who lack cultural competence.

Sara Reed is a Licensed Marriage and Family Therapist and psychedelic research therapist at Imperial College London. She has discussed the potential harm of "psychedelic tourism," where predominantly White facilitators offer psychedelic experiences to communities of color without a deep understanding of the cultural contexts and experiences of those communities. Reed argues that this can lead to a lack of cultural sensitivity and understanding of the unique needs and experiences of Black and Brown people, which can result in harm and even re-traumatization.

Monnica Williams is a clinical psychologist and founder of the Center for Mental Health Disparities at the University of Louisville. She has researched and written about the potential for cultural bias and insensitivity in psychedelic therapy and the need for greater cultural competence among facilitators. Williams has argued that without an understanding of the cultural experiences and systemic issues faced by Black and Brown people, facilitators may unintentionally perpetuate harm or reinforce harmful beliefs and attitudes.

Both Reed and Williams have emphasized the importance of culturally competent facilitation and the need for greater diversity and inclusion within the field of psychedelic therapy. They have called for greater awareness and sensitivity to the unique needs and experiences of people from diverse backgrounds, and for a commitment to equity and social justice within the field.

Another one of my colleagues in this field is Dr. Darron Smith, a public health expert and professor at the University of Memphis. He has also spoken out about the need for greater awareness and understanding of the unique experiences and needs of Black people in the context of psychedelic use. In Dr. Smith's words:

"Psychedelics are not race-neutral. There is a complex social history of drug use, abuse and policy that must be considered before promoting a psychoactive substance that has the potential to exacerbate disparities that already exist in our society."

While this book is written for a broad audience, as a woman of color I personally have felt the difference when sitting in psychedelic sessions with culturally competent facilitators and those who were clueless. It makes a big difference. You can connect with me online for monthly live Zoom sessions in our Sacred Psychedelic Saturdays to ask questions and explore these issues further. Sign up for the link and replays at SacredMedicineStories.com.

Many of the psychedelic substances mentioned in this book are still classified as Schedule 1 in the USA[2], and they are banned by the United Nations Convention on Psychotropic Substances of 1971, which means they are not available for use outside of clinical research trials in most countries. Using underground or street drugs can prove to be harmful, so while our authors have accepted the risk inherent in taking these substances, none of the authors nor the publisher suggest that you take any illegal substance or engage in illegal activity. This book is meant for educational purposes and harm reduction only.

There are several preparation tips that can be helpful before embarking on a psychedelic journey or shamanic ceremony. These are covered in more detail in the *Appendix* of this book. And I invite

---

[2] Schedule I drugs, substances, or chemicals are defined by the US Drug Enforcement Agency as **drugs with no currently accepted medical use and a high potential for abuse.** Some examples of Schedule I drugs are: heroin, lysergic acid diethylamide (LSD), marijuana (cannabis), 3,4-methylenedioxymethamphetamine (ecstasy), methaqualone, and peyote.

you to read James Fadiman's book, *Psychedelic Explorers Guide,* for more in-depth insight into psychedelics.

A short summary of preparation practices for you to consider include:

1. Setting intentions: It's important to set clear intentions for the experience. This can involve reflecting on what you hope to gain from the journey or ceremony and what areas of your life you would like to explore or heal. While you will also be encouraged to surrender those intentions before entering ceremony, the prep work of outlining them helps many people get more out of their ceremonies.

2. Choosing a safe and comfortable setting: The physical environment in which the experience takes place can have a significant impact on its outcome. It's important to choose a setting that is safe, comfortable, and conducive to the type of experience you hope to have. Taking steps to only enter a ceremony or setting where your physical and emotional safety are looked out for can help you relax into the journey.

3. Practicing self-care: Taking care of your physical, mental, and emotional health in the days leading up to the experience is important. This can involve getting enough sleep, eating well, staying hydrated, and engaging in activities that promote relaxation and well-being.

4. Avoiding certain substances: It's generally recommended to avoid certain substances, such as alcohol, sugar, and caffeine in the days leading up to the experience. This can help to reduce anxiety and promote a more positive experience. And some medicine workers suggest specific diets (or dietas)

that include no meat, no sex, no street drugs, etc., to prepare to receive the sacred medicine.

5. Working with a trusted guide or facilitator: Working with a trusted guide or facilitator can provide a sense of safety and support during the experience. A guide can also help to facilitate the journey or ceremony and provide guidance or assistance as needed. Vetting your facilitator to ensure they have no history of abuse is essential, and so is trusting your gut. If your intuition makes you think the person isn't safe or legit, don't sit in ceremony with them.

6. Preparing for the integration phase: It's important to recognize that the experience is not over once the journey or ceremony has ended. The integration phase, during which you process and integrate the insights and experiences gained during the journey, can be just as important as the experience itself. It's important to have a plan in place for how you will integrate the experience into your life in a positive and healthy way.

PART 1
CALL TO ADVENTURE

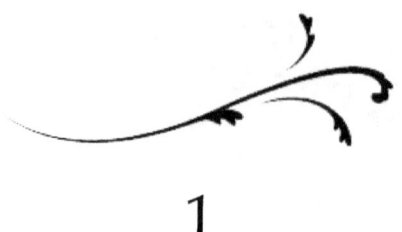

1

The Ordinary World

The Ordinary World is the first stage in the Hero's Journey framework, and it refers to the world in which the hero lives before they embark on their journey. The Ordinary World is our hero's starting point, their everyday life. It is a place of comfort and familiarity, but also of limitation and constraint. In films and novels, the hero is usually shown to be living a mundane, ordinary life, and may be dissatisfied, restless, or yearning for something more. This can be a key motivator for the hero to answer the Call to Adventure and embark on their quest.

The Ordinary World serves as a contrast to the world the hero will eventually enter on their journey. It is a world of routine, predictability, and conformity, where the hero may feel trapped or stuck. It is often depicted as a place where the hero's talents and abilities are unrecognized, and where they are held back by societal or cultural expectations.

However, the Ordinary World is also a place of safety and security, where the hero has a sense of belonging and familiarity. It may be a place of family, friends, or community, where the hero has a support system and a sense of identity. In general, at this opening stage the hero is not yet aware of the Call to Adventure that will set them on their quest.

Overall, the Ordinary World is an important starting point for the Hero's Journey, as it establishes the hero's character, motivations, and the challenges they face. It creates a contrast with the world the hero will eventually enter, and sets up the stakes and potential rewards of their journey.

Examples of the Ordinary World in literature and film include Harry Potter's life at the Dursleys' house before he learns he is a wizard, Luke Skywalker's mundane existence as a farmer on Tatooine before he meets Obi-Wan Kenobi and discovers the Force, and Bilbo Baggins' peaceful life in the Shire before he embarks on his adventure with Gandalf and the dwarves.

For most of us who embark on shamanic or psychedelic journeys, we are often in need of or seeking change but have no idea just how radically our lives can transform. In the Ordinary World we may have heard of psychedelics or medicine men and women with special gifts of healing, but we have no clear path to encounter them. That is, until we hear the Call…

As I mentioned in the Introduction, my Ordinary World was one of sadness and gloom. While I was living as a functional depressive, I was not thriving. As I share in this chapter, my first calling to take a mind-altering substance that wasn't a prescription drug was in 2000 and it was MDMA. This guided me to a new way of seeing myself and what was possible for me.

In our next story by KaRen, we see a distraught military veteran in an everyday life of pain and suffering. KaRen suffered various forms of trauma. She even hit rock bottom which included multiple arrests, alcoholism, and crippling anxiety when a very special dog came into her life. Her service dog, Artemis, along with the sacred medicines of wachuma and ayahuasca, helped her to find healing and set her on a path to helping others.

From Ordinary to Extraordinary
By DaeEss 1Drea Pennington Wasio, MD

Up until my mid 30s I lived with a near constant dark depressive mood and a longing to be free from my pitiful human life. My earliest memory is of being whipped with a belt because I wet the bed. I was only 1 year old.

My parents divorced when I was 3 and my mother moved me and my siblings from Nevada to Colorado. I always attributed my sadness to their divorce and missing my dad. My mother told me that I was the apple of my father's eye. She said he always held me, fed me, and read to me while she was busy with medical school studies. So, I wonder how it must have felt to go from being held, rocked, and sung to in my father's arms each day to seeing him once or twice a year.

When my mother finished her medical training and went into private practice, I was shuffled between babysitters and my older sister. I grew up like many latchkey kids, seeing my mom only in the evenings. On weekends, I went with her to the hospital for rounds and hung out in the gift shop. I was always quiet and well-behaved, especially because I grew up hearing my mother repeat that children were to be **seen**, not heard. Just as she was told growing up.

The conversations with my dad on the phone were mainly about how I was doing in school. He came from a generation that believed that education was the most important way to get a stable job, a pension, and a secure future.

So, when my dad found out I was going to be in a school play or a music recital, I often heard the tone of disapproval in his voice.

13

He told me that my grades were most important and that successful musicians are one in a million.

I worked hard in school to keep my father's approval, so I could keep playing in the band, acting in plays and singing in the chorus. It was through music and theatre that I could channel my bottled-up emotions and it was **on** stage where I finally was told it was both GOOD and acceptable to speak up — and sing out loud!

Of course, dad urged me to focus on my studies so that I could get accepted to medical school. So, I felt the need to hide and downplay my true passions and interests. I didn't want to be seen as not serious.

From childhood to early adulthood, I became a chameleon. I did all I could to look, sound, and behave in acceptable, serious ways. And sadly, I frequently felt overcome with shame and guilt any time the urge for artistic expression bubbled up within me.

I lived for years with an ever-intensifying feeling of unease, never fully comfortable in my own skin, never quite feeling good enough. I was terrified that someone would discover I wasn't smart enough. I rarely enjoyed the fruits of my hard labor — getting all As on a report card didn't make me feel good about myself or confident.

Later the applause for a good performance at work or on stage did not translate to high self-esteem nor pride. My sense of self-worth never increased based on the things I did, but I still tried even harder to be perfect...

It was not a fun way to live. And I frequently felt sad and lonely. I am not exaggerating when I say that a constant feeling of loneliness and melancholy permeated my life. By the age of 13 I had active suicidal plans. I count myself lucky to have found LSD in my later teen years, as I'm convinced that like so many others, it kept me alive and got me through high school.

Awakening to a way out of darkness

In 2001, at the tender age of 30, a friend from medical school saw my relationship patterns and gifted me a book that inspired a deep self-discovery process and initiated my healing journey.

While I understood that my parents' divorce had a huge impact on me, reading *Getting the Love You Want* by Harville Hendrix and Helen LaKelly Hunt taught me how characteristics of both my father and mother imprinted an 'ideal partner' within my psyche. That image was what subconsciously drove me to recreate childhood situations of distance and emotional unavailability in an effort to repair and heal my attachment wounds. This prompted me to face the wounds of my childhood with the help of MDMA.

The gift that my MDMA sessions delivered to me was the felt sense of unconditional love, something I never felt in any relationship — not in romantic relationships nor in my family of origin.

One evening, while listening to chill music, I took some MDMA with a close friend. Within 30 minutes a vibrating feeling of warmth started pulsating from my solar plexus up to my heart, then flowing down my arms. A tingly feeling of joy whisked up to my face, and my jaws felt so tight as I was involuntarily clenching them. Spread across my face was a broad smile like a Cheshire cat.

I felt bliss, love, connection to a force beyond myself. I felt light, relieved, hopeful. MDMA showed me how much resentment I held toward my mother and how it was poisoning my mind. I felt compassion for her, especially as I revisited the stories she told me about her childhood in Guyana. I called my mother that night to tell her that I loved her.

I was awakening to how insidious the programming and stories I believed since childhood were, and how they kept me locked into insecure behavior patterns and emotional reactions that were linked to perfectionism and a compulsive need to prove myself.

I also saw just how little self-love I had. Coming to the realization that I didn't love myself and that I was only acting out unconscious programming prompted me to start searching for help, relief and understanding. I began psychotherapy, attended self-help seminars, entered into deep spiritual practice, and explored the depths of my shadow.

Integrative, holistic healing

Beside my personal healing discoveries, in my growing new medical practice I was also learning how a variety of holistic, complementary, and integrative approaches could bring harmony to body and mind, including helping people overcome depression, anxiety, PTSD and mental anguish linked to experiences of trauma, loss and early life adversity. From breathing practices to creative visualization, meditation, acupuncture, craniosacral therapy, Somatic Experiencing, Thought Field Therapy, and hypnosis alongside cognitive behavioral therapy, nutritional therapy, and health education, I was providing a whole new paradigm in holistic, integrative healing to my patients.

Just a few years after finishing my internship at Georgetown University hospital, I was witnessing my patients progress through deep, lasting transformation in physical, emotional, sexual and spiritual health. Even the clients who came to me for age management awakened to extraordinary levels of wellbeing through stress management, hormone optimization, and conscious life planning.

The science nerd in me was thrilled to find research about many mind-body therapies and modalities showing promise in the treatment of disease and mental illness. So, in my private practice I offered cutting edge integrative treatment, but in my media job on TV I presented watered down, highly edited news reports and documentaries. As the medical director and spokesperson for Discovery Health Channel, every day for many years I was seen on televisions in homes across America.

While my personal spiritual pursuit pointed the way to inspiring possibilities for healing through meditation, mystical experiences, and positive psychology interventions, the conservative TV network wasn't willing to let me share the new science of healing.

Cracking under pressure

A troubling feeling of discontent percolated beneath the smiling, polished surface I portrayed on TV. A battle of truth began between my ego and my soul. A fight for authenticity, integrity and hope created muscle tension, anxious thoughts, and sleepless nights. How could I live with the thought that in my private practice I provided better advice than I could provide to the TV audience?

My moods took a dark turn, something a shaman I would meet in years to come predicted if I didn't learn to live true to my soul. Existential dread and a longing for peace stirred up long suppressed suicidal ideations, but the memory of a voice I heard in my teenage years that inspired me to vow to not kill myself reminded me that I made a commitment to see this life through to its natural end.

As I shared in my TEDx, My Journey to Self Love, by 2005 I had become quite the go-getter. I was driven to build up my credibility through multiple advanced degrees, licenses and certifications. In fact, our family joke is that I have more degrees than a thermometer. But all of the shiny material wealth I earned did not spark any joy. Instead, I had incessant thoughts that nothing really mattered.

I woke up each day feeling sad and totally empty. I dreaded leaving the house. It was only a sense of duty and obligation that motivated me to put on a happy mask, get dressed and rally to enter the daily grind.

I was a functional depressive. Only a few years into my professional career, I'd already published my first book and appeared on the Oprah Winfrey Show twice. I regularly appeared in the media flashing a bright smile from ear to ear. But my smile did not reflect true happiness.

The price of driving myself so intensely, constantly seeking approval gave way to intense feelings of self-loathing and burnout. Like a dark, heavy cloak, depression became a constant presence in my life. It felt as burdensome and constricting as a coat soaked through from the rain, dripping in black sticky tar. That thick weighty cloak of depression had an oversized hood that drooped over my eyes, narrowing and blocking my vision, and it compressed my ears, muffling the rich sounds of life and my own internal music, and it allowed sad thoughts of hopelessness to seep into my mind.

Leaving the ordinary world behind: my out of body experience

In 2005 Dr. William Tedford, to whom this book is dedicated and the co-founder of a continuing education and entertainment travel business, invited me to speak and sing on a cruise along the Mediterranean Sea. This was a welcomed reprieve from the steadily growing doom and gloom overtaking my heart. At the last minute I discovered that my travel confirmation was missed by the organizers, so I wouldn't make the cruise. With a round trip flight to Barcelona already paid for I decided to go on the trip, but not as the medical media personality, Dr. Andrea. I chose to go as *Dreah, the artist*, with a commitment to leave my comfort zone, get out into various cities and sing when and if I were given the chance.

The opportunity first presented itself in Saint Tropez, France when I was invited to sing at a posh disco, and hundreds of chic clubbers swayed and swooned to my jazzy riffs. With pumping bass and flashing lights, I felt exhilarating bliss as the music, the crowd and I became one. It was ecstasy! For the second time in my life I felt love, uplifting, life-affirming unconditional love for myself, the joyful partygoers on the dance floor, and for life itself.

When I woke up the following morning at my hotel in Cannes, I reveled in the memories of the magical night. Reliving the moments of bliss, connection and self-love, I felt a high so pure I questioned my entire reality.

"How is it possible that last night I felt like the real me, as if I was accepted and loved for being me even though no one there had ever heard of me or met me before?" Wonder, awe, amazement and amusement swirled around my brain.

19

Then, realizing that in just two days I'd have to return to the constricted, unfulfilling life I had back in the USA, I burst into tears. The contrast between the life I had and the life I desired was too great. I didn't want that old life, a fact I harbored for many months. Then a rolling wave of dark sadness welled up from my stomach and rushed to my head. I flung myself on the bed, crying loudly and shaking involuntarily. I called on God to take my life.

I said, "Take my life, my business, my body! I don't know what I'm doing with them, and I can't go back to that life!" The shaking of my body led to a deep release as I felt myself melt into and merge with the bed. Suddenly a piercing, bright white light blasted my eye lids. Curious how the sun could possibly get any brighter I opened my tear-filled eyes to find the source of the light.

To my great surprise I found that the light was coming from inside my head! I quickly felt my body peel away from the bed and rise up to the light. I was pulled ever so gently into a tunnel of light and waves of peace enveloped me. A sense of calm so profound permeated every part of me as I ascended to the light. I thought that God must finally be answering my prayer by taking my life. This brought a gentle, peaceful smile to my tear-stained face.

Passing through the tunnel of light I emerged in a sea of oneness, I felt as if I had merged with all that is. I was one with a tranquil, boundless loving energy. Then, a scene appeared in my awareness. It was a review of my entire life. Images flashed before me, taking me from my birth, through childhood to that present day. In an instant I saw so clearly how every decision of my life, whether made consciously or not, led me to the depressive state I endured.

I became instantly aware that I have a choice in life, that we all do. With this realization I felt the kind, gentle presence of a being

20

standing next to my life. I leaned toward it and said, "I had no idea I could choose differently! Now that I know, I could go back." A new vision appeared before me, a vivid scene of me walking playfully hand in hand with a child along the Mediterranean Sea in Cannes. I saw myself living in France, singing professionally, and I saw that I could heal with energy coming from my hands.

In that future vision I was supremely happy, radiant and at peace. Seeing a future so glorious I said yes to life, and I was quickly whisked back into my body lying on the bed of my hotel room. I was infused with a new enthusiasm for life and the depression I had lived with for 30 years was gone.

Within weeks of returning to America I began preparing for a life in France because I believed so deeply in the vision from my out-of-body experience. And then I met the father of my daughter and was soon pregnant with our daughter.

At that point I had never heard of anyone having an out-of-body or near-death experience (NDE) without being in a coma, under anesthesia or in an accident. So, I began to research NDEs and mystical experiences. This led me to explore a variety of indigenous practices and shamanic ceremonies, as you'll read in Chapter 3. You'll also learn more about my move to France and how sacred medicines and shamanic journeys led me to embrace a new identity and become the best mom I could ever hope to be.

MDMA

MDMA (3,4-methylenedioxymethamphetamine) is a synthetic drug that belongs to the class of drugs known as empathogens or entactogens. These drugs are psychoactive substances that are known to produce feelings of empathy, emotional openness, and connectedness to others.

Empathogens like MDMA work by increasing the activity of three key neurotransmitters in the brain: serotonin, dopamine, and norepinephrine. Specifically, MDMA increases the release of serotonin, which is a neurotransmitter that plays a crucial role in regulating mood, appetite, and sleep. The increase in serotonin levels is responsible for the feelings of euphoria and emotional openness that people experience while on MDMA.

In addition to its empathogenic effects, MDMA also has stimulant properties. This means that it can increase heart rate, blood pressure, and body temperature, which can be potentially dangerous in certain situations. It is also known to cause a range of physical and psychological side effects, including dehydration, muscle tension, jaw clenching, anxiety, and depression.

MDMA is a Schedule I drug in the United States, which means that it is considered to have a high potential for abuse and no accepted medical use. However, some researchers are exploring the potential therapeutic benefits of MDMA for treating conditions such as PTSD (post-traumatic stress disorder) and anxiety in clinical trials.

LSD

LSD, or lysergic acid diethylamide, is a powerful synthetic psychedelic that can induce profound changes in perception, thought, and mood. LSD is typically taken orally, in the form of small tablets or paper squares (also known as "tabs" or "blotters") that have been doused with the drug. The effects of LSD can last for several hours, with peak effects occurring after about 2-3 hours.

Many people have reported using LSD as a tool for healing and personal growth. The psychedelic experience induced by LSD can be intense and sometimes challenging, but it can also be deeply transformative and therapeutic. Some of the reported benefits of using LSD for healing include:

1. Increased empathy and compassion: Many people who use LSD report feeling a heightened sense of empathy and connectedness with others. This can help to break down barriers and promote healing in relationships.

2. Expanded consciousness: LSD can induce profound changes in perception and thought, leading to a sense of expanded consciousness and a deeper understanding of the self and the world.

3. Alleviation of anxiety and depression: LSD has been shown to have therapeutic potential for treating anxiety and depression. The drug can help to break negative thought patterns and promote a sense of well-being and positivity.

4. Spiritual experiences: LSD can induce mystical or spiritual experiences that can provide a sense of purpose and meaning in life. These experiences can also promote a greater sense of connectedness with the universe and a deeper understanding of the nature of reality.

LSD is a powerful drug with potentially serious risks and side effects, thus should only be done under the guidance of a trained professional in a controlled setting. Additionally, LSD is illegal in many countries and possession or distribution of the drug can result in serious legal consequences.

Grandfather's Alchemy
By KaRen

My eyelids felt heavy as I struggled to open my eyes while a blinding bright light increased my strain. I felt my eyes fill with tears when I finally opened them. The last thing I remembered was two dark eyes staring at me like two black holes swirling like a vortex in space. I realized that it was because my brain was lacking oxygen while someone tightened their grip around my neck. I remember thinking that was my last breath in this world as I drifted onto complete darkness and welcomed death. To my surprise, that blinding bright light was not heaven but the ceiling lights in my hospital room when I awoke the next day.

I told myself that was the end of an abusive cycle and the beginning of a healing one. However, I had no idea what that was, what it would look like, or how to begin. I spent days, weeks, months, and years suffering from post-traumatic stress, chronic migraines, and many associated fears and symptoms from that experience, trying to regain control over an unmanageable life. I had just returned from a combat deployment a few months before and was also experiencing a sense of detachment from who I was. During my entire time in the military, I'd felt a constant identity crisis because I hadn't been able to be who I really am, and I struggled to connect with myself.

All this compounded trauma was followed by an alcohol dependency, multiple arrests, financial distress, deteriorating health, crippling anxiety, and many other physiological disorders including psychosomatic seizures. As a conditional release from jail, I was escorted to a military rehab facility. That was the first time I had ever spoken to a mental health specialist and marked the beginning of my healing journey.

Soon after I was released from inpatient therapy, I returned home but was still dealing with agoraphobia because I found myself living in constant fear for my life. It was a very dark and depressive period in my life where I felt hopeless, helpless, forsaken, broken, and suicidal.

That's when Artemis came into my life. She was a Belgian Malinois dog. Divine timing aligned for us both. She slowly helped me to feel safe since I would sometimes sleep in my bathroom as a panic room. I was not even bathing because I felt vulnerable in the shower. I was angry, abrasive, and tired, and believe it or not I was still in denial and refused help, drinking myself to blackouts to combat insomnia.

I slowly started to feel safe enough to sleep and shower and even leave my house with Artemis because I trusted her to have my back. I saw her as a protective measure and a deterrent, at first. However, over the years, I began to build on our bond and I started to *FEEL* again after years of numbing myself to escape my reality. She slowly taught me about *unconditional love*, being there for me even through my worst phases. Even when she would be the receiver of my anger she was there, patient and loving.

I grew up without any real knowledge of emotional intelligence. No one ever sat me down to talk about my feelings and explain what and how emotions affect us. Don't get me wrong, I was loved and hugged, but my parents were busy and struggling to make ends meet. This conversation was simply not part of my life because it was also not a part of theirs. But it's up to us to break generational traumas by recognizing these patterns and building awareness around them to shift them toward a more intuitive and compassionate approach.

Losing Artemis, an invitation to sacred medicine

Over the years after I left the military, I decided to retire Artemis because I had found profound healing in having her as my support. I attended retreats and therapy, I traveled abroad, socialized differently, and found healthy ways to cope with my symptoms. I went back to school, volunteered as a veteran peer mentor, became a strong advocate by helping raise awareness, and even helped develop a post-traumatic growth program. I attribute all of it to her devotion and earthly mission to help me.

The manner of Artemis' accidental death was greatly my responsibility and I felt tremendous guilt about it. A suffocating agony that tugged my heart toward a bottomless pit of despair. I could not breathe, I could not think, I could not calm my nerves. I relapsed back into unhealthy patterns. Losing her left me alone and I spiraled down into a dark abyss, not sleeping, having anxiety attacks, chronic migraines, and depression lurking in the corner. I knew I needed to snap out of it but none of my coping skills were enough.

My friend lived in Peru at the time, and she invited me to sit in ceremony with Wachuma. I bought a ticket the same day. I was eager, I had a million questions, and I had weird expectations. My former experiences with psychedelics had been very raw and rough. Violent purging and wild physiological sensations with crazy visuals had been the norm. I had used psychedelics before in a recreational setting but never in a ceremonial sacred space or a therapeutic setting.

Wachuma was not like that. He was gentle. I felt a warm embrace from the medicine and immediately felt Artemis' energy present. I closed my eyes as I journeyed and spent a beautiful time with her and Wachuma by my side. Playing, chatting, crying, and expressing love in all forms. She slowly transformed into a beautiful luminescent maiden dressed in all white and told me that she was part of my soul family, coming down when I most needed her, and that I didn't need her any longer. She said I was ready to embark on my journey without her. Artemis told me that she is always there, and I can call on her whenever I need her.

I knew I could not dishonor her legacy by allowing myself to lose control of everything I had worked hard to build in my life. We spent the afternoon reconnecting with that frequency of unconditional love, allowing me to process my grief one emotion at a time. When it was time to let go, I was encouraged to release emotion through my heart. Guided by the breath, and full of love, I sent the energy back to source. I did this repeatedly…placing my hands on the earth, I became one with source and allowed myself to release this stagnant energy through my physical, energetic, emotional, mental, spiritual, and ethereal bodies. A full spectrum healing blessing!

I thanked Pachamama and Grandfather Wachuma for holding space for me to do so with every breath. I noticed a lot of other stagnant emotions coming up and getting in the queue to be released. With a deep exhale, I surrendered to the flow and opened my heart gates wider. I lay down on the grass knowing I was held, I was acknowledged, I was healing, I was loved, and I am whole.

Wachuma is different for everyone, but it's known as heart medicine because it allows you to open your heart to release and receive. It's an opportunity for you to reconnect with your heart.

The heart is the key to alchemy; through the heart you can transmute anything into whatever you want it to be. It's an amazing power that's often overlooked and misused. We tend to build more depression, anxiety, anger, and fear by holding these inside when we have the amazing power to release and transform all these energies with the heart.

Master sacred plants help guide us back to our heart space and divine essence, so that we may remember how powerful we truly are. They help me have a frame of reference whenever I am feeling lack so that I can tap into the ever-flowing fountain that lives within my heart to replenish my spirit and continue to thrive.

Embracing a new calling

I have since returned to Peru to continue working with the medicine. I have connected with Grandmother Ayahuasca as well as other plant medicines, but Wachuma continues to be my most favored. In January 2021, I found myself helping to facilitate ceremonies in Cuzco. Grandfather's voice came in strong and told me that I needed to share my experiences with others as well as the medicine itself. I never really considered that I would be serving the medicine and holding space for others in ceremony. This new calling felt foreign at first.

Many insecurities and self-limiting beliefs came up. I needed to get out of my own way to align with my life path. I continued to ask Grandfather day in and day out, "How was *I* supposed to do all that?" While in Cuzco, I learned how to prepare the medicine through a sacred guided process, and he placed me in situations where he would guide me and provided me with confidence in my innate ability. I realized that I am not the one healing; the medicine does the healing. My job is to open my heart and allow its guidance to flow through while supporting others through their own self-realization and self-actualization journey.

Over a period of synchronicities, I found myself attending psychedelic-assisted therapy seminars and courses to expand my understanding, training, and capacity to continue exploring the medicines in a therapeutic setting as a treatment for post-traumatic stress as a complement to my Mind-Body Medicine Master's Degree program.

Today, I am honored to co-facilitate retreats for both veterans and civilians with a focus on post-traumatic growth. There's still a long journey ahead but for the first time in a long time, I feel I am fulfilling a purposeful mission: one that targets healing from a multidisciplinary approach and helps raise collective awareness through empowerment.

A'ho!

ABOUT THE AUTHOR

KaRen is a Marine combat veteran who continues to serve as an ambassador, volunteer, and advocate for several veteran service organizations invested in the wellness of veterans and their families. She is an author and continues to expand her education with a degree in Mind-Body Medicine. KaRen is a certified Cognitive Behavioral Coach, Integrative Nutrition Health Coach, Warrior Goddess Training Facilitator, Reiki Master, and is currently working on her trauma-conscious yoga teacher training.

Inspired after experiencing struggles with post-traumatic stress and military sexual trauma symptoms for years, she embarked on a holistic wellness journey and found a path of choosing meditation over medication. KaRen discovered that she was missing a balance of the "Healing Trifecta" of mind, body, and spiritual engagement. She has made it her life's mission to embody resiliency to inspire others to transcend their trauma and limiting beliefs.

KaRen's published journal, *Mastering Alchemy: A Journey of Cultivating Power From Within*, can be found on Amazon.

Connect with her on Instagram: @sacredowljourney

Wachuma

Wachuma, also known as San Pedro, is a psychoactive plant that has been traditionally used for spiritual and medicinal purposes in the Andean region of South America for thousands of years. It contains mescaline, a powerful psychedelic compound that can induce altered states of consciousness, introspection, and emotional exploration.

Many people who have used Wachuma in a therapeutic context report that it can help with the healing of depression and trauma. The experience of Wachuma is often described as being deeply introspective and emotionally intense, allowing individuals to explore their innermost thoughts and feelings in a safe and supportive environment.

During a Wachuma ceremony, participants are often guided by an experienced shaman or facilitator who can help them navigate the experience and provide support as needed. The ceremony may involve chanting, drumming, or other forms of ritualistic practices to enhance the spiritual and emotional aspects of the experience.

Some research suggests that the use of Wachuma in a therapeutic context may be effective in treating a range of mental health conditions, including depression and trauma-related disorders. One study, for example, found that individuals who participated in a Wachuma ceremony reported significant reductions in symptoms of depression and anxiety, as well as improvements in overall well-being.

It's important to note, however, that Wachuma is a powerful psychoactive substance and should only be used under the guidance of an experienced and qualified practitioner. It can also have potential risks and side effects, such as nausea, vomiting, and psychological distress, especially when used improperly or without adequate preparation and support. As such, anyone considering Wachuma as a therapeutic option should first consult with a qualified healthcare professional and seek out reputable and experienced practitioners.

2

The Call to Adventure

The Call to Adventure in the Hero's Journey can be seen as a metaphorical initiation of a personal transformation journey. Feeling called to take psychedelics or enter shamanic rituals and ceremonies can be similar in several ways.

First, they both involve a sense of inner restlessness or dissatisfaction with the current state of one's life. The Call to Adventure in the Hero's Journey is often triggered by a sense of being unfulfilled or called to something greater than oneself. Many people who feel called to take psychedelics or enter shamanic rituals and ceremonies may feel a sense of dissatisfaction or disconnection from themselves, others, or the world around them. This feeling of disconnection can motivate people to seek out experiences that can provide them with a deeper sense of meaning, purpose, and connection. Similarly, feeling called to take psychedelics or enter shamanic rituals and ceremonies can be driven by a desire for spiritual or personal growth or a yearning for a deeper understanding of oneself and one's place in the world.

Second, both experiences involve a willingness to step outside of one's comfort zone and embrace the unknown. The Call to Adventure in the Hero's Journey requires the hero to leave their ordinary world and embark on an exploration of new territory, where they will face challenges and may undergo personal death and rebirth. Similarly, taking psychedelics or entering shamanic rituals and ceremonies can require one to let go of familiar ways of thinking and experiencing the world, and embrace a more expansive and unfamiliar perspective.

Finally, both experiences can be seen as opportunities for personal growth and transformation. The Call to Adventure in the Hero's Journey and taking psychedelics or entering shamanic rituals and ceremonies can both offer insights into oneself, the world, and one's place in it. They can help to break down limiting beliefs and patterns of thought, expand one's sense of self and the world, and provide a deeper understanding of the mysteries of existence.

Of course, it's important to note that taking psychedelics or entering shamanic rituals and ceremonies should always be approached with caution and respect, and under the guidance of a trained and experienced practitioner. The Hero's Journey in psychedelic and shamanic ceremony can be a transformative path for personal growth and evolution, but not every individual will experience it in the same way or at the same pace. Ultimately, it's up to each person to decide whether or not to answer the Call, and how to navigate the challenges and opportunities that lie ahead.

In our first story in this chapter by South African author, Valencia Khoza, we learn how she left depression behind and began to walk in peace and joy thanks to sacred medicines. After a lifetime of appeasing others to keep the peace, Valencia learned wisdom from a series of mentors and teachers. She realized that mainstream antidepressant meds weren't working and decided to try ayahuasca. Enjoy reading her colorful experiences while under the influence of this Amazonian plant medicine.

In our second story in this chapter by American author, Andi Wagner, we see that she felt drawn to attend a retreat in Costa Rica to try plant medicine despite her misgivings. While initially against it, she'd been convinced by her teenage son to try it. Ultimately ayahuasca helped heal her depression and gave her a new lease on life.

Basic Human Tales
By Valencia Tsakani Khoza

Every one of us experiences a constant state of death and rebirth. Every experience evokes survival techniques that we unconsciously prioritise. From a very young age, I developed the habit of appeasing others to keep the peace.

Between the ages of three and five, I allowed my father to molest me. I say 'allow' because it was our little secret as he would indicate with his index finger on his mouth to not say a word about it. I later found out that my other siblings had the same experience with my father who was their alcoholic stepdad. I felt uncomfortable being left completely alone with him because I thought the molestation would go beyond just a finger in my vagina. Luckily, I was never alone. The experience continued even after my parents separated. When I reached my teenage years, I decided to stop visiting him. This was due to the deliverance services attended at church. Enough was enough. I called it a miracle.

You see, like many of us, I was born out of wedlock. I was carried by a divine feminine who, in this lifetime, had only experienced ruptured relationships. From her mother departing from the physical realm when she was only three years old, to being raised by aunts and stepmothers with whom she found it difficult to relate. She yearned for unconditional love, and she perceived any sign of kindness as an invitation to believe 'this is the love I have been longing for.'

Many of these experiences were short-lived. My mother's temperament would manifest in negative ways and friends, family members and romantic partners didn't like her constant need for validation and dependency. She was like a child who still needed a parent and never got the chance to become an adult except through the inevitable growth of giving birth to us and being labelled as a mother. She was my first teacher.

I saw her pray daily asking God to provide for her or take her life. These ultimatums created a distorted relationship between me and God. It made me believe that we can tell God what we want and when we don't get it, we can continue collecting karma as He doesn't care about our suffering.

Observe, learn and unlearn

Throughout my upbringing, my family was my motivation to keep going. As the youngest of two elder sisters, I have learned so much from them and hope to share this wisdom with my younger brother. My brother was born autistic and how we communicated truly unlocked a deeper understanding of uniqueness. In instances when he felt misunderstood and lashed out, my family trusted that I'd help calm him down as it was easy for me to understand his needs. Just by picking up his energy, it was as if I could hear and deliver what he required.

The downloads of new thoughts leading to a change in my understanding were always silent and gentle. They wouldn't happen in deep sleep or trance, just gentle knowing at a given moment. Like whispers which made me respond with a whistle. I was confused and cautious because I didn't understand what it was.

In many instances, I would disregard these gentle teachings. I chose in my mid-teenage years to not engage or listen further. I thought, 'This is false. I need to be in a trance to get access to all this information.'

38

I didn't leave it at that though; I did private online research and kept myself informed through numerology and seeking my life path. Still unfulfilled, I started seeking mentors. To my surprise, the teachers who had answers to my daring questions were not people I could connect with face-to-face. They would be teachers I found through books I read, talk shows, seminars, or conferences I attended.

My greatest teachers were people I met daily. They had these wonderful messages I needed to hear. Many of them opened me up to intuitively share insights. I wondered, who is in charge? It wasn't me. These episodes of knowing and not would sink me into a deep depression when I yearned for answers I couldn't find. I was in therapy from 2013 until 2020 as I knew I couldn't bear the feeling of not having anyone I relate to and constantly being met with being misunderstood.

I grew up having a confrontational approach which got me into a lot of challenging relationships. I had to question whether the truth I am expressing is only my truth or the universal truth which was to be expressed. I suffered internally and ended up having to journal everything privately as the advice and techniques granted by the therapist couldn't resolve the perceived abnormalities. Being normal has always been a challenge.

Paradigm shift; activation

In 2020, my mother passed from a long-standing illness while on prescribed medication for HIV. I also started noticing that the depression medication I was on in 2020 for about 4 months wasn't helping me with anything but was just suppressing any feelings I had. After my mom's death, I asked for an alternative form of healing. Speaking and medicating wasn't helping anymore.

I needed that substance I'd read about during my life path search when I'd typed into Google, 'how to know God on a deeper level'. The search results had told me I needed ayahuasca. In one article, it was said that this Amazonian plant medicine would bring me all the answers and healing I needed.

I was fascinated by indigenous lifestyles. I would daydream about being in a rainforest surrounded by trees and animals. I had a vision of a tree house next to the riverbanks, and my mother was a white snake with green and yellow eyes. I then chose to study a course on zoology and human physiology at university which I didn't complete because I felt I wasn't good enough. I thought, 'What if they find out that my interest comes from the wishful thinking of saving animals and healing the human body by changing how we engage with the external?'

The journey was so exhausting, as I kept on feeling I would never be able to explain what I was aiming at and why. I sabotaged myself somehow and didn't complete my studies. Despite that, I still realised that education is vitally important, especially when you acquire skills aligned with your life path.

Conceptualised downloads

Living in Soweto, I felt a beautiful, divine pull to the Earth. The pull made me trust that my kind was nearby, I just had to open myself up to meeting them. On the 27th of December 2020, three days after we'd laid my mother in her final resting place, my twin flame asked if I would like to go with him and his little sister to a healing retreat. I agreed to go, with some hesitation of course, as it was going to be a whole new experience.

The space was on a mountain and had Rastas, Jews, Shamans and Gypsies alike. On arrival, we were introduced to marijuana and its benefits were explained. There was a fire ceremony accompanied by Golden Teacher psychedelic mushrooms. The next day we hiked after drinking San Pedro, then we went into the sweat lodge. The medicinal journey was amazing. The euphoria I felt was similar to an experience I'd had while sun gazing where I'd felt I was being pulled into the Light. Fear and self-doubt left me. I felt a sense of belonging.

My curiosity and desire to experience ayahuasca led me to ask the group I was with whether they knew about the medicine. They advised me that the medicine would find me, especially since I was calling for it. They said, 'what you seek is seeking you'. I was told that Shamans from Peru as well as the Amazon frequently visited South Africa and they ensure a ceremony is held before they return home. They told me the location could be shared with a select few. I waited patiently for four months, and the ceremony finally happened on the 24th of April 2021.

Cups of wisdom

The day of the ceremony came and I was nervous, yet ready. I thought it was going to be held outdoors near a river or under ancient divine trees. To my surprise, everything happened in a yoga studio that belonged to a Reiki healer. The Shaman seated us in a sequence. On the feminine side, we didn't have fire and were mostly freezing throughout the ceremony.

41

We opened up with setting intentions and passing the Santa Maria, (an alternative name to call the marijuana plant in Portuguese) before ingesting Santo Daime. The first cup was served. 'Delicious', was all I could say after my first sip. Somehow my thirst was quenched. I felt the cells of my body rush to access and absorb the medicine. While listening to the shaker and singing from the *I Am Discourse* book, visions of the last sight of my mother before she'd passed presented themselves. Our life experiences went past quickly yet profoundly. The moments of our lives when she'd cared for me and times when I'd felt neglected. Her strengths and weaknesses were perfectly displayed and how parts of my traits have inherited this particular archetype of victimhood and 'poor me' character.

I understood the messages and felt deep compassion and forgiveness. She was then surrounded by other females who embodied her and me but from alternative timelines. The feminine beings were powerful and held high standards. Truly, that view awakened my confidence. The smell of the burning incense and the toning down of the music brought me back from my journey. Funnily enough, I was participating in the singing and dancing while having a mystic experience. Talk about multidimensional access!

The second cup was offered. I noticed that I was drinking from the same cup. Joy rushed in and affirmed that the Universe has got me. I redirected my gaze to my twin flame who winked but quickly approached me looking like my father. I knew the journey had begun.

My father's face was full of remorse as he knelt and asked for forgiveness. 'I am imagining all this', I thought. The whole room became filled with other masculine beings, some whose faces I recognised and some I couldn't. I felt as though I was one of them at some moments. I saw the wounds and the magic. I felt their strength, I felt safe again and honoured.

My twin's presence was restored, and he was surrounded by a forest and lions in Europe. It was an interesting scene. I scanned the room and all the continents presented themselves in form and significance. I felt a deep sense of belonging. Again, the music stopped, but the happiness and love in my heart were amplified. I walked into the kitchen during the break. I met a Russian/German man who smelled like a restaurant and all sorts of ice-cold alcohol. He slithered his tongue and I felt welcomed. He affirmed my presence and two white rabbit coffee mugs identical to the one I use at the office were on the kitchen counter. I saw this as an affirmation of my significance.

The third cup was prepared, and I couldn't wait. This time to get the same cup I had previously, I stared at it as the Shaman was serving. He picked up my intentions and started playing a game with me. It was so much fun and affirming. Deep heartfelt bows were exchanged when he handed me the third cup. Page 111 in the *Discourse* book opened up.

We started with the invocations on the page. A vision came to me once more: on my left the Earth's Minerals, Ocean, Travellers, Fairies, Satan, and upfront the Messiah on his left Jah, Allah, Jungle, Humans, Distraction, Oppression, and Victimization overseen by Asia. To my right a Gogo and Lions. The status of the Earth was discussed and all of us were assigned to the mission. I felt wings and lightness on my back and feet. Dance and joy ended wars. Families reunited with their tribes and there were blessings all around. Sustainable living where artificial intelligence was an extension of human intelligence. Tranquillity and ease in each soul. Sickness eradicated by eating well. The power of self-sufficiency manifested.

New thought and DNA sequel

'Consciousness can only be achieved through loving wholeheartedly', I affirmed on my knees, bowing and surrendering. Once again, the Messiah called me back to the council. I felt trust for the very first time. God felt like all of us with the shame and misconceptions falling away. I saw poverty, sexual immorality, ill-thinking, jealousy, and judgment melt away. I saw Jah realizing he had to hold hands with Allah and the Messiah to connect with Buddha. The connection for unity consciousness excluded no one and humans were what the mission was all about. The Gogo and the Lion fostered the Earth; beauty and food emerged surrounded by water. Crystal stones and flying things with magical features were brought to light; life was the only desire.

Existence made sense. I am human and I am here right at this moment with these beings, singing and dancing while feeling cold wishing we could at least switch sides with the masculine and sometimes falling behind while reading through the pages of the invocation book. We felt so naughty and had moments of being called into order which was done lovingly and gently. Playfully sharing everlasting wisdom on how we can use science, philosophy, and commerce to live peacefully with nature and the entire universe. Currency eventually was eradicated and integrity, devotion and accountability were defaulted behavioural traits. Lightness was achieved after trusting conscious breathing. It was evident that life was made possible in thin air. 'We have to be what we expect to see in others. What they are, can only be who we are. But how could that be when everyone is uniquely made and has a purpose they must also fulfil?'

Everything else became a question that required an answer. Depression and anxiety flashed away. I understood I had nothing to fear, nothing to worry about and definitely nothing to be ashamed of. I was made with due care and full intentions. I was in position and holding my now-becoming-cold water bottle and my toes were freezing. Some participants in the ceremony were sleeping, purging, and singing out of tune. That was it – the ceremony was at its end.

Revelations were brought forth. Insights into my life path were presented with ease. From that point on, I was functioning on a different vibration which I appreciate until this day. A shift in perspective took place. I realised that this is what I had always known but hadn't stayed in this conscious state of being. I knew that all was well. There was peace in my heart.

The kitchen filled with chefs and jolly beings. Laughter was the order of the day. Gladness found all of us delighted and sane. We shared the journey and found that many of us had been connected throughout the entire time. In our hearts we had determination to walk the Earth knowing we are guided and supported. We all knew how worthy, important, and valuable we are. We're equally as valuable as the elementals, nature spirits and cosmic beings are. We honored the material world and valued its manifested forms. Artificial intelligence is just human intelligence coming from Source.

About The Author

Valencia Tsakani Khoza is a grid and lightworker from Soweto, South Africa. She appreciates utilizing what is in front of her by communicating her behavioural observations. She's a devoted lifelong student of human conduct, using her life experiences. She trusts that human engagements are far beyond relation, ethnicity, calibre or habitant. 'A force within us is creating our reality that we mainly choose to react to instead of surrendering to co-creation.'

As a seeker, she acknowledges that each individual reflects another viewpoint of who we truly are. She has seen how competition and thriving for power have devastated humanity and personal conduct. Her work is intuitive and requires presence, devotion and acceptance of collective individuality and our own conscious emotional maturity. These are attainable through conscious heart-opening movements and breathing.

Ayahuasca

Ayahuasca is a psychoactive brew that has been traditionally used for spiritual and medicinal purposes by indigenous communities in the Amazon basin of South America for thousands of years. It is made by boiling the Banisteriopsis caapi vine and combining it with the leaves of various other plants, typically Psychotria viridis or Diplopterys cabrerana, which contain the psychedelic compound DMT.

The effects of Ayahuasca are often described as being deeply transformative and spiritually profound, inducing a range of psychological and physiological effects such as altered perception of time and space, vivid visual and auditory hallucinations, introspection, and emotional exploration. The experience typically lasts several hours and is often accompanied by nausea, vomiting, and diarrhea.

In recent years, Ayahuasca has gained popularity in the Western world as a potential tool for spiritual growth and personal transformation, as well as for the treatment of a range of mental health conditions, including depression, anxiety, PTSD, and addiction. However, it is important to note that the therapeutic use of Ayahuasca is still a controversial and relatively unregulated area, and its safety and efficacy as a treatment modality have not yet been fully established by scientific research.

Furthermore, Ayahuasca is a powerful psychoactive substance and should only be used under the guidance of an experienced and qualified practitioner. It can also have potential risks and side effects, such as psychological distress, anxiety, and the exacerbation of underlying mental health conditions, especially when used improperly or without adequate preparation and support. As such, anyone considering Ayahuasca as a therapeutic option should first consult with a qualified healthcare professional and seek out reputable and experienced practitioners.

Santo Daime

Santo Daime is a syncretic spiritual practice that originated in Brazil in the early 20th century. It combines elements of indigenous Amazonian shamanism, Catholicism, and African religions, and centers around the ritual use of a sacramental brew called Ayahuasca, which contains the psychedelic compound DMT.

Santo Daime ceremonies involve singing hymns, dancing, and drinking Ayahuasca in a group setting, led by a trained spiritual leader known as a "mestre". The experience of Ayahuasca is often described as being deeply transformative and spiritually profound, allowing individuals to access deeper levels of consciousness, gain insights into their personal issues, and connect with a sense of higher purpose or meaning.

Many people who have participated in Santo Daime ceremonies report that it can be helpful in the healing of depression and trauma. The experience of Ayahuasca is often described as being deeply introspective and emotionally intense, allowing individuals to explore their innermost thoughts and feelings in a safe and supportive environment. It can also help to facilitate emotional release, allowing individuals to work through past traumas and emotional blockages.

Research on the therapeutic use of Ayahuasca is still in its early stages, but preliminary studies suggest that it may have potential benefits for the treatment of a range of mental health conditions, including depression and trauma-related disorders. Some research suggests that Ayahuasca can increase the production of brain-derived neurotrophic factor (BDNF), a protein that plays a key role in the growth and survival of neurons and has been linked to the treatment of depression.

It's important to note, however, that Ayahuasca is a powerful psychedelic substance and should only be used under the guidance of an experienced and qualified practitioner. It can also have potential risks and side effects, such as nausea, vomiting, and psychological distress, especially when used improperly or without adequate preparation and support. As such, anyone considering Ayahuasca as a therapeutic option should first consult with a qualified healthcare professional and seek out reputable and experienced practitioners.

Ayahuasca Changed My Life
By Andi Wagner

I firmly believe everything happens for a reason. The people we meet, the jobs we accept, and the experiences we have all happen for a reason. There are no coincidences. The author, Squire Rushnell wrote a book called, *When God Winks*. In it, he calls "Godwinks" divine coincidences to seize certainty in uncertain times and acts of God's enduring love.

It was no coincidence that I was called to go to a Life Advancement Center in Costa Rica that offers ayahuasca ceremonies, there were too many Godwinks calling me.

First came the mushroom trip

A few of my friends had told me about their experiences with 'shroom trips and ayahuasca, but I'd never thought much about it. It didn't interest me; I thought the only way to work through our childhood trauma and emotional issues was in therapy.

I hadn't entertained the thought of plant medicine and I was actually against it completely, until my 17-year-old, my only son, came to me pleading to allow him to do a trip. My son, who I now realize is my teacher, was feeling depressed. He was still holding in all his emotions from our divorce when he'd been 12 years old. He was angry with his dad for falling in love with a woman (with six kids) and moving on. He was also taking his anger out on me. When he was with me, life under my roof wasn't enjoyable. He was being a disrespectful teenager and I was being a frustrated, nagging mother. Something had to change.

51

He attempted to tell me how psilocybin mushrooms were being used to help patients with depression, anxiety, and PTSD and how he could benefit from a trip. To support his case, he sent me YouTube videos on 'shrooms, LSD, DMT, kambo, and breathwork including a Netflix documentary, How to Change Your Mind, based on the same book written by Michael Pollan. It explores the history and uses of psychedelics.

I watched, I learned, and I agreed. It helped my son. He was happier and softer and his relationship with me and his father improved. I was grateful for the trip; I was a believer.

I remember seeing my massage therapist and not knowing why but asking him if he had ever taken ayahuasca. He told me that he had been in over 200 ceremonies and firmly believed in its magic. He also suggested that I only go somewhere where I would feel safe – not into the Amazon by myself. He mentioned a center in Costa Rica and I left and forgot about it.

About three months later, a friend phoned me to tell me about his amazing trip to Costa Rica where he'd experienced ayahuasca. Now my ears perked up. Twice I'd heard the name of the center and ayahuasca. That night I Googled the center and booked my retreat for November. I can't explain why but I just knew I had to go there. This was the retreat I had been looking for in past seven years since my divorce.

The breakdown

After my son had left for his first year at CU Boulder, I was alone in my house for the first time. I was an official empty nester. I'd been divorced for three years and separated for three. My ex-husband was marrying the mom-of-six, and my uncle, who's like a father to me, had just fallen and broken his hip. He lived in Pennsylvania, in my childhood home, and I was his caretaker. One could say that I was holding a very full plate. Looking back, I wasn't fully aware of how much it was affecting me emotionally.

Depression had its tight grip on my throat, and I couldn't breathe properly anymore. I was at a point in my life where I lost my sense of self. I was numbing myself with tequila (the best choice for the least painful hangovers) marijuana edibles and Ativan to sleep at night — weed, sex and late-night parties. I no longer recognized the face staring back at me in the mirror. I was feeling emotionally, psychologically, and physically unhealthy. I was getting monthly yeast infections, UTIs, canker sores, gut issues, and conjunctivitis. Louise Hay, author of, *You Can Heal Your Life*, believed all our physical ailments are directly correlated to what's going on with us emotionally.

I was feeling depleted and exhausted. As a mother, it pains me to admit this, but I was also having suicidal thoughts. I knew I needed help, but I didn't want to take the route of antidepressants and occasional therapy sessions didn't alleviate the depression and feeling of being overwhelmed. I had tried antidepressants in the past – Wellbutrin, and Zoloft – but they'd left me feeling like a zombie, merely masking the underlying psychological issues like a cheap band-aid.

I didn't know how to help myself.

Sad clown

We all have two personalities. One we show to the world, our Instagram account, friends, and family, and the one we keep hidden behind the "Judy Jetson" mask. As a kid, I remember watching The

Jetsons, which was a cartoon sitcom about a family living in the future. Judy would answer her futuristic video call (now our FaceTime) in the morning and look like hell – Wren and Stimpy eyes, messed up hair, and still in her robe. She would grab her "mask" that looked like the perfect image of herself with coiffed hair and made-up face. I was also wearing my mask and it was wearing me down.

Thank God I'd picked up a second career when my son was nine. I'd followed my dream of being an actress at the ripe age of 48 and thankfully had been booking commercials and Lifetime movies regularly. My work kept my mind off my reality. I could walk on set, turn it on, live my character's life, shoot my scenes, and go home. However, when I entered my dark, empty house, I'd again feel the weighted blanket of sadness, loneliness, and despair.

The brew

I like to call ayahuasca "White Magic." It changed my life, opened my mind, gave me insight into my past and it healed me. Ayahuasca is a plant medicine. It's a brew made from the Banisteriopsis caapi and Psychotria Viridis plants. It has hallucinogenic properties that are mediated by DMT (dimethyltryptamine) in your brain. It's been around for thousands of years and originated in the Amazon for spiritual and religious purposes. It's also used in Brazil and Colombia. Traditionally a shaman or an experienced healer leads an ayahuasca ceremony.

Ayahuasca affects the central nervous system, leading to an altered state of consciousness that varies from person to person. Some people will experience hallucinations, out-of-body experiences, ego death, and euphoria. This is usually accompanied by purging – vomiting, pooping, spitting, burping, and the release of mucus.

It helps to open your mind, heal from past traumas, and as I learned at Rythmia, merge you back with your soul and heal your heart.

I went to the retreat to uncover sexual childhood trauma I'd had a feeling about but never truly known the truth about. The idea of using plant medicine to eradicate depression intrigued me and I was willing to try anything to escape the consistent feelings of sadness. I needed a week away to save myself; a week of self-healing and mothering myself with organic food, massages, colonics, breathwork, yoga, and ayahuasca ceremonies.

My story

I never met my birth father. My mother was on her third marriage when she had me at 34 years old. For reasons I'm still unsure about, she was unable to care for me after my father deserted us so when I was six months old, my maternal grandparents became my legal guardians. They were in their mid-60s and had already raised three children of their own. I would often hear my grandfather say, "If it weren't for you, we would be traveling the world." He wasn't the warmest man in the world, and I can remember seeing him hitting my mother when I was eight years old and then punching my grandmother in the face when I was 14 years old.

My grandparents were snowbirds. They owned a house in the Pocono Mountains in Pennsylvania and a home in Pompano Beach, Florida. Every November, we would pack up the car and head out for a three-day drive to the warm south. Each night before my grandfather would pull into the cheap motel called the Days Inn, he would instruct me to hide behind his seat. I remember tucking myself into a tiny ball, like a scared little hamster hiding under its straw bed, pretending to be invisible so the man behind the motel desk wouldn't see me and possibly charge my grandfather more money for having a child. That's when my lack of self-worth was born. I wasn't worth the extra money it might have cost and I shouldn't be seen or heard. I had to just pretend I didn't exist and disappear.

The trip

Trying to explain exactly what I experienced in Costa Rica during my ayahuasca trip would be like trying to explain to someone who's never given birth what it feels like to be pregnant and in labor.

Everyone's journey is completely different and unique.

While I was under the influence of plant medicine, I was amongst 73 other souls all on our individual mattresses complete with a bucket for vomiting and a roll of toilet paper to wipe tears or blow our noses. One night I blew through an entire roll of toilet paper from just blowing my nose.

When we purge, we release the energy of the past – trauma from our childhood as well as our ancestors' trauma. Anger, resentment, sadness, and anything we may be hoarding in our bodies will surface and come up and out.

I've never cried harder or longer in my life. Personally speaking, one night of ayahuasca was like ten years of therapy.

The first night I experienced what is known as a "consulta." This is when you hear "spirit," "God," "Mama Aya," or your inner voice speaking to you. The following is what I heard:

"I know you think you came here to uncover your childhood trauma but I called you here for a different reason. Thank you for hearing the call and listening. You have cancer in your left breast. Do you want to live or die? If you want to die, the cancer will spread rapidly; if you want to live, I can promise you your life will be beyond your wildest dreams in the best possible way."

I know, it sounds crazy. I felt crazy and I didn't want to believe I had cancer cells growing in my breast. I spoke back to "the voice" and, after some deliberation, decided I wanted to live. I was told that I needed to still get a mammogram upon my return home. Mamma Aya assured me that I would be cured by the end of the week. She told me not to worry.

At the end of the night, we were encouraged to share our experiences with the group. I was hesitant but knew if I were to believe I had cancer, I would have to say it out loud, so I shared.

After the last night in the ceremony, which was an all-nighter, one of the other participants who knew I was concerned about my cancer came up to me and said that he was compelled to share a message. He said, "Andi, you don't have to worry, your cancer is gone. I had a dream that I was standing next to you and we were hugging, and I felt and saw golden energy moving from my body through your body. You don't have to worry." I have no way of proving whether or not I had cancer cells, but I had a mammogram on January 19 and the results came back negative. I was truly relieved because two years prior a puckering had been found in my left breast and I'd been required to get an MRI.

On the second night of the ceremony, Mama Aya told me that it was time to forgive my aunt, my mother's sister. We'd had a strained relationship for over 25 years and hadn't spoken for almost eight years. Only recently, because of my uncle's fall, we'd been forced to text because our calls had always been riddled with anger, dissonance, and arguments.

Mama Aya told me to reach into my aunt's chest and pull out her heart. Once again, it seemed crazy to me what I was feeling and experiencing, but I went with it. I was told to look at the heart in the palm of my hand. I felt a stone-cold heart and saw it was black and dead. At that moment, I felt so much compassion for my aunt and what she must have felt as a child. I knew her childhood had also been riddled with pain.

I was told to send love to her dead heart and to breathe on it as though I was bringing life back to a baby bird that had fallen from its nest. As I did this, I literally felt the warmth and weight of a heart that was pumping with fresh blood again. I felt it coming back to life and this brought a smile to my face. I was then instructed to place her heart into mine. When I did this, I felt the love of forgiveness and compassion. I immediately felt as though a weight had been lifted like a boulder that had been pressing down on my ribs.

The lessons

Ayahuasca showed me that every person, experience, and situation in my past had led me to where I was because we are all interconnected; we are all energy.

I learned to trust my inner voice and to stop looking for approval outside myself. We already have all the answers inside us, we simply have to be still and listen.

I received clarity and knowledge about what happened to me as a baby and toddler. I can now move forward and leave the shadows behind me.

Since I've returned home, my emotions are stable; mentally I'm stronger and feel more grounded than I have in years. I'm less reactionary and feel more in touch with my softer, feminine side. I no longer suffer from long bouts of depression. My ADHD is more manageable and spiritually I'm more mindful and have a much clearer understanding of loving my fellow brothers and sisters on this planet. I see the world and people through a clearer lens, with more compassion and patience.

Ayahuasca ripped open my mind and my heart and reconnected me with my soul. I was told to get rid of certain people from my life and I did. In some ways, what I was being told and shown I'd already been feeling on a subconscious level but had refused to listen.

During all my trips, I experienced intense happiness and bliss but also experienced terror and felt unbearable emotional pain and frightening darkness. I learned so much about my life and myself that I'm still processing all that came up for me. I feel already called to go back to Costa Rica for more self-discovery and transformation. It's not for everyone, but for those of you who enjoy running into the storm at full speed, listen for the call.

About The Author

Thanks to a wicked mid-life crash at the age of 48, Andi decided to leave the dishes in the sink and abandon domesticity for the stage as a stand-up comic. She wrote parenting and marriage jokes for over two years and appeared at The Comedy Store, The Ice House, Flappers, and other comedy venues across Los Angeles. Andi landed an agent, and her childhood dream of becoming an actress came true.

Andi was no stranger to the world of entertainment. For 15 years she worked behind the camera casting and segment producing for various dating, game, reality, and talk shows. She credits her daily meditation and hot yoga practice for keeping her grounded and present. Her joy comes from hiking in the Santa Monica mountains, stand-up paddle boarding, and traveling. Her purpose and passion are inspiring others to become the best versions of themselves and never give up on their dreams.

Connect with Andi on Instagram: Andiwagner11
Follow her film and TV career: www.IMDB.me/andiwagner

3

Refusing the Call

Not everyone who hears a call or feels the urge to try psychedelics immediately says yes. Whether it's due to fear, poor timing, or lack of resources, one may have to refuse the call to sit in relationship with a master teacher — whether in the form of fungi, plant, or human.

Refusing the Call is a stage in the Hero's Journey in which the hero initially resists the Call to Adventure and tries to avoid or ignore the challenges and opportunities that lie ahead. This stage can be seen as a form of resistance to change, as the hero may be afraid of the risks and uncertainties that come with embarking on a new path.

Similarly, refusing to take psychedelics can also be seen as a form of resistance to change. Psychedelics can be a powerful tool for personal growth and transformation, but they also involve risks and uncertainties that may make some people hesitant to try them.

Some reasons why people may refuse to take psychedelics could be:

1. Fear of the unknown: The psychedelic experience can be unpredictable and intense, and some people may be afraid of what they might encounter during the trip.

2. Social stigma: Psychedelics are still illegal in many parts of the world and are often associated with counterculture and drug use. Some people may be reluctant to try them because of the negative stereotypes and stigma associated with their use.

3. Personal beliefs: Some people may have religious or moral objections to the use of psychedelics, or may believe that they are not necessary for personal growth and transformation.

4. Lack of access: Psychedelics are not widely available and may be difficult or expensive to obtain, especially if one does not have connections within the underground community.

However, just as refusing the call can ultimately lead to stagnation and regret in the Hero's Journey, refusing to take psychedelics can also mean missing out on the potential benefits of the experience. By facing their fears and taking the plunge, the hero and the psychonaut alike can open themselves up to new possibilities and experiences that can lead to personal growth, transformation, and a deeper understanding of themselves and the world around them.

Of course, it's important to note that the decision to take psychedelics should never be taken lightly, and should always be approached with caution and respect for the substance and its effects. Likewise, the Hero's Journey is a metaphorical framework for personal growth and transformation, and not every individual will experience it in the same way or at the same pace. Ultimately, it's up to each person to decide whether or not to answer the call, and how to navigate the challenges and opportunities that lie ahead.

Entering Into Relationship with Ayahuasca
DaeEss 1Drea Pennington Wasio, MD

Just one year after the birth of my daughter, I heard the initial call to sit with the Great Mother Ayahuasca. It was in 2007 while attending a trance dance workshop in Sedona, Arizona. During the workshop the shaman taught us how many indigenous cultures around the world hold rites of passage rituals and ceremonies to help their community members embrace their new roles and responsibilities as they entered into new phases of life. In some shamanic settings, one sees clearly how we move along a trajectory of ego development, into finer levels of self-actualization, and ultimately self-transcendence.

The shaman explained how modern pursuits of notoriety, status, money and possessions have replaced indigenous ways of being, ways that are tied more to nature and respect for life. I came to see how it was not just my broken home, but also the colonial, patriarchal, capitalist society I was raised in that also led me to feel so lost and sad.

I came to understand that I had to break free from the person I had been molded and folded into to discover and become who I was truly meant to be, my Authentic Self. I was curious to learn more about the shamanic practices of soul retrieval our facilitator knew of, so I asked him. One way to facilitate that unlearning process was to sit with ayahuasca. Our shaman explained that he leads ayahuasca retreats in the jungles of Hawaii.

As you read in Andi and Valencia's stories in Chapter 2, ayahuasca is a psychoactive brew that has been used for centuries by indigenous people in South America for spiritual and medicinal purposes. It is made by brewing the Banisteriopsis caapi vine and other plant ingredients, often including the leaves of the Psychotria viridis plant, which contains the psychoactive compound DMT (dimethyltryptamine).

Ayahuasca is often consumed in a ceremonial setting, guided by a shaman or healer. The effects of the brew can last for several hours and can include intense visual and auditory hallucinations, as well as feelings of deep introspection and emotional release.

Our shaman told us how many people who have used ayahuasca report that it has helped them to gain a deeper understanding of themselves and their place in the world. The intense experiences that can occur while under the influence of ayahuasca can help individuals to confront and process their fears, traumas, and other psychological blocks that may be holding them back in life.

The introspective nature of ayahuasca experiences can also lead to profound insights about one's purpose, values, and beliefs. Many people report feeling a greater sense of connectedness to others, nature, and the universe as a whole.

Purging with ayahuasca

The shaman cautioned that the use of ayahuasca is not without risks. The intense and potentially overwhelming nature of the experience can be difficult to navigate for some individuals, and the use of ayahuasca can also interact with certain medications and health conditions. Plus, one of the common effects of ayahuasca is purging, which can involve vomiting, diarrhea, sweating, and/or salivating. This is often referred to as "la purga" or "the purge" and is considered to be an important part of the healing process in many traditional ayahuasca ceremonies.

The mechanism behind purging is believed to be related to the interaction between the active ingredients in ayahuasca and the body's natural defense mechanisms. The Banisteriopsis caapi vine contains MAO inhibitors (MAOIs), which can prolong the effects of DMT and other psychoactive compounds found in the brew.

MAOIs work by inhibiting the activity of monoamine oxidase, an enzyme that is involved in the breakdown of certain neurotransmitters, including serotonin, dopamine, and norepinephrine. By inhibiting this enzyme, MAOIs allow these neurotransmitters to remain active in the brain for longer periods of time, leading to the intense effects of ayahuasca.

One theory behind purging is that the body's natural defense mechanisms are triggered in response to the presence of the MAOIs and other psychoactive compounds in ayahuasca. This can cause the body to try to expel these substances through vomiting, diarrhea, sweating, and salivating.

In traditional ayahuasca ceremonies, purging is often seen as a necessary part of the healing process, as it is believed to help release negative energy and emotions from the body. However, it is worth noting that not all individuals who use ayahuasca will experience purging, and the experience can vary widely depending on the individual and the specific brew of ayahuasca being used.

The thing that turned me off was when the shaman explained that in his ceremonies in the Hawaiian jungle, participants would take the brew at night, and they'd have to dig their own holes for puking and shitting. The idea of being on a hallucinogen at night, in the jungle, which was inhabited by all sorts of wild animals and creepy, crawly venomous creatures, with a bunch of strangers where I would likely lose control of my bowels while facing my deepest fears and traumas, shut down my curiosity and led me to say no to ayahuasca.

Hearing the call — again

Nearly 10 years after that initial call, I felt a new desire to enter into relationship with what some call the Great Mother or Grandmother, ayahuasca. She is known as a master teacher of several master plants which are believed to be teaching allies for healing, development and evolution of humans. I was ready to take my personal evolution journey to the next level and explore ways to undo some of the negative programming that was impacting my parenting.

Learning more about ayahuasca made me think I was ready for a gentle teacher. Ayahuasca is considered to have a feminine spirit or energy. In my research I found that there are several reasons why ayahuasca is associated with the feminine:

1. Nurturing and healing energy: Ayahuasca is believed to have a nurturing and healing energy, similar to that of a mother or grandmother. This energy is thought to help guide and support individuals through their healing and transformational journeys.

2. Connection to the earth: Ayahuasca is a plant medicine, and as such is believed to have a deep connection to the earth and nature. This connection is often associated with feminine energy, as the earth is often personified as a mother or caregiver.

3. Spiritual wisdom: Ayahuasca is also believed to possess spiritual wisdom, similar to that of an elder or grandmother. This wisdom is thought to come from the spirit of the plant itself, as well as the ancestors and spirits that are invoked during the shamanic ceremony.

4. Empowerment: The grandmother energy of ayahuasca is also associated with empowerment, as it is believed to provide individuals with the strength and courage to face their fears and overcome their obstacles.

Overall, the feminine energy of ayahuasca is seen as a powerful and transformative force that can guide individuals through their healing and transformational journeys. It is often seen as a compassionate and nurturing presence that helps to facilitate growth and personal evolution. This knowledge inspired me to commit to sit with ayahuasca when given the right opportunity.

In 2017, while on a spiritual retreat in Peru, I was given an opportunity to attend an ayahuasca ceremony performed by a beautiful ayahuascera. She was a petite medicine woman who came from a long lineage of healers in Peru, having trained in serving this potent brew in the jungles of her native land. She and the musicians wove together a deeply moving experience of sound and spirit that gently brought me into relationship with ayahuasca that I'll always treasure.

I was initially quite nervous that my experience would be filled with vision of demons or scary images. Instead, within 45 minutes of drinking my first cup, I was welcomed by a matrix of colors and shapes that appeared as a beautiful kaleidoscope that seemed whimsical and playful. Listening to the beautiful icaros, songs of the ayahuasca tradition, I felt safe to let down my vigilant, fearful stance.

Icaros, magical songs of healing

Icaros are traditional shamanic songs that are sung during ayahuasca ceremonies and other psychedelic journeys in South America. These songs are believed to have a powerful and transformative effect on the participants, and they're an essential part of the healing process.

The word "icaro" comes from the Quechua language, which is spoken in the Andes region of South America. Icaros are typically sung by the shaman or other experienced facilitators during the ceremony, and they're often accompanied by various musical instruments.

There are many ways in which icaros can help to support psychedelic journeys and facilitate healing. They help in setting the intention. Icaros are often sung at the beginning of the ceremony, and they can help to focus the participant's attention and provide a clear direction for the experience.

Icaros help create a safe and supportive environment as well. The music and singing can create a sense of safety and support for the participants. The shaman or facilitator's voice can provide a grounding presence that helps to guide and comfort the participants during their journey.

Icaros are also believed to have a powerful and transformative effect by enhancing the psychedelic experience and opening up new levels of consciousness. The music and singing can help to deepen the journey and provide a sense of connection and unity. The singing can help to navigate difficult emotions or experiences, providing a sense of direction and purpose. And Icaros are believed to have a healing effect on the participants, helping to release emotional blockages and promote physical and mental well-being.

The singing can create a space for emotional release and provide a sense of closure and resolution that a simple playlist cannot.

Speaking to my mother s soul

The songs soothed me and as I relaxed into the mattress, the geometric shapes gave way to images of familiar scenes from my childhood and the face of my mother. Despite being separated by thousands of miles and an ocean, I sensed my mother so close to me. At that time her cognitive faculties and memory were far from the feisty, brilliant woman I admired.

In that altered state I spoke to my mom, thanked her for giving me life. I apologized for the unspoken anger and disappointment I harbored. My heart burst with compassion and grief. I cried — no wailed — as I grieved the loss of my mother while she was still alive.

I also saw my sister who was mom's primary caretaker. I felt immense guilt penetrating my head and heart as I wailed on. Sobbing into my pillow, using so much toilet paper to blow my nose, I fully gave myself to the process as I wrung out my whole being, finally facing the sadness I felt and hopelessness that plagued me.

I was surprised to hear a message of tenderness from a place that was both within me and beyond me. I was told that the situation was exactly as it should be based on agreements my mom and sister's souls made before entering this life. I understood that despite my best efforts I could not improve of change their dynamic, that it is their karma that must play out.

After sobbing a bit more, saddened by the recognition of my need to surrender, I felt the deeply held grief lessen its grip on my heart. Accepting life as it is and my power to change only myself led to more peaceful energies permeating my being. I left the ceremony with a greater sense of acceptance and compassion for myself and my family. I felt blessed to have had the time to do such a deep dive into my past and felt renewed to live more peacefully in the present.

Returning home, I felt empowered and grateful to have a new relationship with this great master plant. And I knew it would not be my last journey. As you'll read in Chapter 9, my relationship with ayahuasca has continued to this present time, and led to profound healing, releasing and ultimately being reborn!

PART 2
INITIATION

4

Meeting the Mentor

In the Hero's Journey, the Meeting of the Mentor is a pivotal stage in which the protagonist encounters a wise or experienced figure who provides them with guidance, advice, and support as they begin their journey. This stage occurs after the hero has made the decision to embark on their quest, but before they begin their journey in earnest. The Meeting of the Mentor marks a transition from the ordinary world to the world of adventure and transformation.

The Mentor is often someone who has already completed a similar journey or has a wealth of knowledge and experience that can help the hero navigate the challenges and trials ahead. The Mentor may be a teacher, a friend, a spiritual guide, or even a supernatural entity. This Mentor may be a physical person, such as a wizard or a wise elder, or they may be a spiritual or symbolic figure, such as a deity or an animal guide.

The Mentor serves as a catalyst for the hero's journey, providing them with the tools and knowledge they need. During the Meeting of the Mentor, the hero may be reluctant or hesitant to accept the Mentor's guidance, but ultimately recognizes the value of their wisdom and experience. The Mentor may offer the hero a gift, such as a magical object or a piece of knowledge that will aid them on their journey. They could offer a magical talisman or weapon, provide them with training or advice, or offer words of wisdom to help them build confidence for the road ahead. By accepting the Mentor's guidance and assistance, the hero acknowledges their own limitations and begins to prepare themselves for the challenges ahead.

Importantly, the Mentor is not a substitute for the hero's own agency or responsibility. The hero must still face their own challenges and make their own decisions, but the Mentor can provide guidance and support along the way.

Here are a few popular Meeting of the Mentor references in literature and film:

1. The wizard Gandalf in J.R.R. Tolkien's *The Lord of the Rings* serves as a mentor to Frodo Baggins, providing guidance and assistance as he embarks on his quest to destroy the One Ring.

2. In the Disney film "The Lion King," the character Rafiki serves as a mentor to Simba, helping him to overcome his fears and embrace his destiny as king.

3. In the novel *To Kill a Mockingbird* by Harper Lee, the character Atticus Finch serves as a mentor to his daughter Scout, teaching her important life lessons and helping her to understand the complexities of the world around her.

4. In the film "The Matrix," the character Morpheus serves as a mentor to Neo, teaching him about the true nature of reality

and helping him to unlock his full potential as the chosen one who can save humanity from the machines.

5. In The Empire Strikes Back, the second installment of the Star Wars saga, Luke Skywalker travels to the planet Dagobah to seek out the legendary Jedi Master Yoda, who becomes his mentor and teaches him the ways of the Force.

6. In The Karate Kid a teenage boy named Daniel moves to a new town and becomes the target of bullies, he meets Mr. Miyagi, a wise and patient martial arts instructor who becomes his mentor and teaches him the skills he needs to defend himself.

The Mentor may not be someone you meet personally. They could come in the form of a book, like this one, or in a documentary, a podcast interview, or a chance meeting at a coffee shop. The relationship with the Mentor may be fleeting or last a long time. In either case, they provide just the right nudge, inspiration or education to get you going on your journey.

In our next story by American author, Kathy Hill, a meeting with a special guide led Kathy to explore new ways of healing. A heroic journey of exploring shamanism ensued. Kathy had a torrid upbringing and then as an adult was given a possible multiple sclerosis diagnosis. On top of this, she lost her mother and beloved dog. Her discovery of shamanism and experiencing a "miracle moment" of soul healing and wholeness is inspiring.

Miracle Moments
By Kathy Hill

I had just been told that I might have multiple sclerosis. The
nagging pain and burning in my feet appeared to be more than just
over-exercise. When I heard the doctor's words, my heart started
pounding and my body froze. I was an active, single woman, living
alone without any family. What would this mean for my future? Was
I going to end up in a wheelchair? I was scheduled to pick up a
puppy in the morning – she was going to help heal the hole in my
heart from losing both my mother and beloved English springer
spaniel. I had already picked out a name and was in love with her
brown freckled face. Should I still get her?

My mind was racing. Pacing around my bedroom, I cried out to
God, asking Him to give me a sign. If getting her was the right thing
to do, I asked to see a hummingbird. I had never seen a
hummingbird in the many years living here, so knew it was an
unrealistic request. I walked downstairs, resigned to the fact that I
would need to call the breeder and say I was not coming. Entering
the sunroom to get the phone, a flash of blue-green caught my eye
outside the window. It couldn't be, could it? A tiny hummingbird
with wings flapping faster than anything I had ever seen, hovered at
eye level, looking at me. How do things like this happen?! I fell to
the floor and cried. God had just spoken to me, and I knew I was
going to be alright.

A few months earlier, I had been sitting with my mother during
her last hours, thinking every breath would be her last. I asked God
for another sign. My heart was breaking, and I needed to know that
we were not alone – that God was with us. I turned on the TV to

break the silence and saw Wayne Dyer in his PBS special saying, "If you knew God was standing over your shoulder in this very moment, how would it change things?" It changed everything! Once again, God had spoken to me. I refer to these experiences as synchronicities or "God moments" and have been blessed with many. A few years later, I had another that I refer to as my "miracle moment." Before I share that story, let me set the stage.

> *"You are alone and all one – all at the same time"*
> *Wayne Dyer*

My family blueprint

I spent most of my life feeling alone and trying to figure out where "home" was, where I belonged. I grew up in a traditional household and knew that I was loved, but that love felt very conditional. My mother was traumatized after losing her alcoholic mother when she was sixteen, and she carried this addictive pattern into her own life, relying on alcohol, cigarettes, and Xanax to get through. Keeping her happy became my number-one priority.

My father lost his dad when he was seven and grew up on an Army base with his mother. He learned the importance of being strong, not showing emotion, and living by the rules. As an only child of these two parents who were also only children, I felt very alone and like I was always walking on eggshells.

From the outside looking in, our lives appeared to be ideal, but I spent many nights hiding under the covers, listening to angry voices and what I later learned was my mother rocking and banging her head against the wall under her makeup table. Should I ask them to stop because they were scaring me, sneak out and run to a friend's house, or just pull the covers over my head and wait until morning? I always chose the latter, hardwiring the "freeze" response into my body at a very early age.

In high school, my grades were above average – mostly A's and B's, with an occasional C. When a C came home, I was grounded without any discussion. My high school guidance counselor told my parents that I was not "college material" and suggested they enroll me in any school that would take me. I applied to several and was accepted to a university from just my application, without an interview or even going to visit. I remember standing in our kitchen on the harvest gold vinyl floor, being told that this was where I was going. I promised myself at that moment that I would excel in school and become financially independent, so I would never have to rely on anyone for security again. That promise became my mantra.

Over the next twenty years, I graduated magna cum laude, became a top salesperson for a large technology firm, got married, built a house with a three-car garage and marble floors, joined a country club, and started my own executive search firm. I had recreated my parent's lives, which is exactly what I said I did not want. My house even had a similar floor plan to the one I grew up in – this realization shocked me. I had been so focused on trying to prove my worth, that I had designed a life based upon what my parents considered successful. I started to have panic attacks, which was my body's way of saying "pay attention." Something must change.

The search

I dove headfirst into trying to figure out what I wanted. I went through a divorce, made several career changes, attended Al-Anon meetings, got into therapy, learned to meditate, practiced yoga, and explored different spiritual paths. The more I learned, the more passionate I became about wanting to help others "figure out their purpose in life;" to live lives that honored their authentic selves. I became a life/career coach and started leading workshops, teaching classes, speaking at conferences, and working with clients all around the country. I had found my purpose and was loving it, but a sense of "home" still eluded me.

What was I looking for? What did I need in order to "feel at home?" I knew the answer was more about an internal feeling than a place. After losing both of my parents, I found myself without any family or a place that felt like home. There was a hole in my heart, and I did not know how to fill it.

A therapist suggested that I make an appointment to see a shaman. For this conservative Irish-Catholic girl, a shaman felt like a huge stretch but I had not found the answers I was looking for elsewhere, so maybe it was time to try something new. And something new is what led to my "miracle moment."

My shamanic experiences

I drove out into the country, to a small house in the woods where Pat met with her clients. There were windows on all sides of the house, giving the illusion that you were outside when in session with her. She asked to hear my story, wanting to understand what brought me to her work. I shared my background and told her that I was looking to fill the hole in my heart and find a sense of home. I felt very alone and was carrying a lot of anxiety in my body.

She led me over to her massage table, where I laid down and was covered with a blanket. Placing stones on each of my chakras, she moved around the table, chanting, shaking rattles, holding feathers, and blowing something into the air called Florida Water. I loved the smell of the water and sensed her energy was very healing. After spinning a pendulum over each of my chakras, she told me that my throat chakra was very congested. It was holding onto many unspoken words. She asked me to yell – to shout out these unspoken words. I could not do it. Even whispering, the words would not come. The promise I had made to myself to never be loud and angry like my mother, was clearly still in place.

Guiding me to relax, Pat said she would yell for me. She moved around the table, using her strong, deep voice to shout about the nights I hid in bed, the times I was punished for things I did not do, the responsibility I had taken on to make everyone happy, the times I was told there was something wrong with me…

My body started to shake uncontrollably. Both of my arms and legs were twitching, my torso was jumping up and down on the table, and I could not stop it. Aware that our time was almost up, I panicked. I was not going to be able to get up and walk while shaking so violently. Pat assured me that this was my body's way of releasing old emotions and she would stay with me for as long as it took. Twenty minutes later, a sense of calm came over me, followed by deep exhaustion, and then I felt energized and much lighter. There was something magical about shamanism and I wanted to learn more.

Pat invited me to a workshop she was hosting, led by Sylvia, a shaman from Lake Titicaca in the Andes Mountains. Sylvia was coming to North Carolina and in addition to the workshop, she was offering individual sessions. I immediately signed up for the workshop and a soul retrieval session, having no idea what a soul retrieval was. Something inside of me knew that this was exactly what I needed.

In the workshop, I learned that shamanism is an ancient healing tradition and a way of life. It is a way to connect with nature and all of creation. In addition to being a shaman, it surprised me to learn that Sylvia was Catholic. That got my attention. Could I be Catholic and practice shamanism too? This gave me permission to explore shamanism without feeling guilty – a Catholic trait I had mastered and held on to, even though I no longer attended church.

In utero

On the day of my soul retrieval, I drove to Pat's house and found a trailer parked in the driveway. This is where Sylvia was holding her private sessions. I knocked on the door and Sylvia greeted me with a big smile, dressed in her bright red skirt and flowery blouse. She invited me in and asked me to sit at the table, where I found a glass of water, coca leaves, and a stack of stones. Sylvia is an expert in the ancient art of reading coca leaves for healing and this is what she would be using for our session.

She spread the coca leaves out on the table, moving them around for several minutes, and then shared that the leaves had several messages for me. The first was that I had some sort of "wounding" in my sacral chakra, my uterus. She asked if I had lost a baby, had an abortion, not been able to have a baby, or had trauma to my uterus. At first, I did not connect the dots but then realized there were several truths here.

When I was very young, my step-grandmother was babysitting and touched me inappropriately when I was in the bathtub, telling me that I was a dirty girl and men would hurt me. I do not remember much more but my mother later told me that I ran out of the house crying and did not speak for several weeks.

My mother was told when she got pregnant that she and I would both die if she carried me to term. She had unsuccessfully tried to get pregnant for seven years, due to uterine issues. Feeling like the pregnancy was a miracle, she decided to go ahead with it. They took me by C-section six weeks early and we were both in the hospital for quite some time. The doctor told her that he did not believe in God, but this birth made him realize that something much larger was going on than science could explain. He said it was a miracle.

After release comes healing

These fit with Sylvia's coca leaf reading. She said the leaves were telling her that something inside of me still wanted to be born. I was intrigued.

She then moved on to say that my wounding was a spiritual wounding, not a physical one. When we hold onto fear in our spiritual bodies, our physical bodies can get sick. This is what was happening to me. If I healed my spiritual wounds, I would not end up in a wheelchair. I felt a huge weight lift from my body.

Sylvia laid the stones out on the table and instructed me to pick them up individually, thinking of a time when something happened that might have caused a part of my soul to split off. It could have been a big trauma or something small – anything that caused me pain. I was to blow a memory into each stone, saying "Kathy, I love

83

you, I need you, please come back." I did not think I would have enough memories to blow but once I got started, they came flooding back. When I finished, she wrapped the stones in a piece of paper, instructing me to keep them under my pillow for seven nights. Then I was to bury them in my yard.

Driving away from Sylvia's trailer, I was aware that something had dramatically changed. I felt like I was floating. Any discomfort in my body was gone, colors were brighter, sounds were crisper, and my heavy mood had lifted. I heard a voice in my head say, "Pay attention to the land – your answers are in the land." I had no idea what this meant, but I knew it was important. I called Pat to share my experience and she said, "This is what it feels like to be whole – your soul parts have come home."

This Miracle Moment allowed me to feel "one with all" – just like Wayne Dyer said. I no longer feel alone. When I connect with the land, I get out of my head and into my heart, which is where I find my answers. I am still on a journey, but it has become a magical one.

About the Author

Kathy Hill specializes in helping people through career and life transitions. With over twenty years of coaching experience, she works with individuals in one-on-one and group settings, and leads workshops and webinars. Her signature class is "Exploring Your Life Mission," where she guides participants to create a mission statement for their lives/careers.

Kathy graduated magna cum laude from Northeastern University in Boston, with a BS in business administration. She was a top sales producer for several Fortune 100 firms in the technology industry, receiving recognition trips around the world. She was also voted an "Outstanding Young Woman of America."

Realizing her life's purpose was to help people, she opened a highly successful executive search firm that provided career counseling and recruiting services. Her passion for helping people grew and she now focuses exclusively on coaching individuals through career and life transitions.

She can be reached at kathyshill@aol.com or +1 336-740-5915.

Surrender in Psychedelic Journeys

Surrender is a key aspect of the psychedelic experience because these substances can induce profound alterations in perception, cognition, and emotion. When people consume psychedelics, they often feel a loss of control and a sense of surrender to the experience. This can be challenging for some people, especially those who are accustomed to being in control of their thoughts and emotions.

Learning to surrender and trust the process can be helpful for people who are exploring psychedelics. This involves letting go of resistance and allowing oneself to fully experience whatever arises during the journey, without judgment or attempts to control the experience. Surrendering can also help people to overcome fears and limiting beliefs that may be holding them back in their lives.

One way to learn to surrender and trust the process during a psychedelic journey is to set intentions before the experience. This can involve reflecting on one's goals and hopes for the journey and visualizing oneself letting go of any resistance or fears that may arise. Additionally, focusing on the breath and staying present in the moment can help to cultivate a sense of surrender and openness.

It can also be helpful to work with a trained guide or therapist who can provide support and guidance during the journey. A guide can help to create a safe and supportive environment, offer reassurance and guidance when necessary, and help to integrate the experience afterwards.

Ultimately, surrender is an important aspect of the psychedelic experience that can lead to profound insights, healing, and transformation. Learning to surrender and trust the process can be challenging, but with practice and support, it is possible to cultivate a sense of openness and receptivity that can enhance the journey and facilitate personal growth.

5
Crossing the Threshold

Crossing the threshold in the Hero's Journey is a critical moment when the hero moves from the ordinary world into the unknown world of adventure and transformation. This can involve physical, emotional, or psychological changes, and often involves a sense of risk and uncertainty. Similarly, taking psychedelics or entering into a shamanic ceremony can also be seen as crossing a threshold into an altered state of consciousness, where one is able to explore the depths of the psyche and the mysteries of existence. This can involve a profound shift in perception, as well as a sense of risk and uncertainty.

During the threshold stage in the Hero's Journey, the hero typically encounters challenges and obstacles that test their resolve and force them to adapt to their new environment. Similarly, taking psychedelics or entering into a shamanic ceremony can also involve facing difficult and uncomfortable experiences, such as encountering aspects of oneself or the world that were previously unknown or suppressed.

However, the threshold in the Hero's Journey is also a time of growth and transformation, as the hero gains new skills, knowledge, and perspectives that enable them to navigate the challenges of their quest. Similarly, taking psychedelics or entering into a shamanic ceremony can also be a time of personal growth and transformation, as one gains insights into oneself, the world, and one's place in it.

The altered state of consciousness induced by psychedelics or shamanic ceremonies can offer a profound sense of connectedness to oneself, others, and the natural world, just like it did in Kathy's story in the last chapter. This can help to break down limiting beliefs and patterns of thought, expand one's sense of self and the world, and provide a deeper understanding of the mysteries of existence.

However, it's important to note that taking psychedelics or entering into a shamanic ceremony should always be approached with caution and respect, and under the guidance of a trained and experienced practitioner. Crossing the threshold in the Hero's Journey and entering into an altered state of consciousness can both involve facing the unknown and the potential for discomfort or danger. It's up to each individual to decide whether or not to answer the call and cross the threshold, and to do so with care and intention.

In our next story by Jamie Church, we see how crossing the threshold by taking psilocybin for past trauma led to the resolution of longstanding guilt and shame. When the COVID-19 pandemic hit, Jamie was already emotionally and physically low. Her strong Christian background didn't seem to help. Weekly online appointments with a therapist helped somewhat but it was only after micro-dosing with psilocybin that she experienced a breakthrough and could come out of her dark cave. She was able to find freedom from her depression and the abuse and trauma that had caused it with multiple psilocybin journeys.

Out of the Cave and into the Garden
By Jamie Church

It was 10 p.m. and I was walking down a busy residential street, contemplating walking into traffic. I was sniffing rock bottom and scared of what was coming. For a large part of my life, I had felt as if I'd been fighting the darkness of depression. Some days I was above it and functioning like a normal mid-30s stay-at-home mom of three; I was happy enough, social enough, doing enough to get by, and fighting my demons decently. But that gravitational pull downward was always there waiting for me to weaken enough that it could grab me and bring me down to the depths.

In the spring of 2020, as the pandemic set in, I could feel my strength rapidly getting sucked out of me. I was facing the same stressors as many others–cut off from family (the US/Canada border between us and my parents was closed), my two elementary-aged kids attempting to do virtual school, and a 2-year-old toddler at home, in total social isolation.

My body was in rough shape. My weight had crept up to the highest ever and I was desperately uncomfortable all the time. I was not sleeping, either due to my own anxieties or my children waking up multiple times in the night. Not only was daily life difficult but I could also feel trauma from the past wriggling under my skin, threatening to break through.

I had worked hard on keeping my past at bay, telling myself it had been dealt with – how could it not be? I had been a devout Evangelical Christian for many years, a missionary even. I had gone through Christian counselling programs, read hundreds of self-help books, and forgiven and let go of hurts and hang-ups. Yet, here we were again as if none of that had mattered. In fact, I had let go of all my belief in anything at that point. I had deconstructed my faith away from Christianity completely over the few years leading up to this time in life and felt like I was truly on my own in the universe.

In the winter of 2021, I found myself in my darkest months. Due to the urging of friends and my husband, I pursued counselling and connected with an amazing therapist online. Talking with her felt simultaneously terrifying and relieving. I would talk to her while lying in my bed in the dark with my headphones on and my eyes closed. She was like this little voice in the distance that I slowly opened up to, and I let myself be heard. Those weekly appointments were a little life raft I would cling to that kept me from sealing myself up completely, and I used them to keep me moving forward.

In the spring, my friend Jeff mentioned to me that he was going to an art experience and bringing "magic mushrooms." I laughed and asked, "Where the heck are you getting those?" I was shocked to hear that they were in a legal gray area in Canada and easily bought online. He texted me the website and I didn't think much about it again until a few months later when Jeff tragically passed away. As I was scrolling back through our conversations, I found the website he had given me and out of curiosity, I clicked on it. I was opened up to a new world that day. The website explained the therapeutic benefits of psilocybin and micro-dosing, and I devoured the info.

I started micro-dosing in mid-August and had begun to notice an opening of emotions that I hadn't felt before, like it was showing me cracks in the hard shell I had created around my psyche. By this time, I had thrown myself into research on the therapeutic use of psychedelics and was aching to try an actual trip with a higher dose;

I could feel the pull of something greater. I talked it through with my therapist who had kept an open mind about the whole thing, but it was all new to her as well, so she advised me to proceed with caution.

I planned to meet with her after doing it so I could debrief my experience, an important and invaluable part of the process, I've come to find. My first trip was a small dose but was enough to open up my mind and allow me to see an absolutely life-changing view of past trauma. That was the beginning of what I see now as my total healing from two very life-changing events.

Awakening the inner healer

From the age of 14-16, I'd been deeply entwined with the family of my church youth pastor, babysitting for them regularly and spending many hours a week in their home. It had been an unhealthy dynamic from the start and unfortunately ended with him sexually abusing me. Six months later on a snowy day in January, I was driving with my best friend and two boys from my church on the way to a youth retreat. As we rounded a bend in the road, my car slipped on the ice and we slid into oncoming traffic. The impact was so great it had split my car completely in two halves, taking the lives of both boys in the back seat. Both events had shaken my family and church community, leaving me reeling and struggling through the rest of my senior year of high school.

After graduating, I moved to Vancouver to join a Christian missionary organization and start a new life. I tried to move on from the past, but the effects of those traumas tormented me slowly and quietly throughout the years, and it's no surprise looking back now that my mushroom journey would bring me back to these experiences.

During my first trip, my mind took me back to the day when I first told someone that sexual abuse had been happening. That day had set in motion a chain of events that I was able to watch unfold in my mind, opening up new memories I had not thought about in over 20 years. I watched my 16-year-old self come home from youth group the night after telling Mitch, the new youth pastor, what had been happening, knowing that my life would never be the same from that point forward. I saw myself collapse into bed, becoming enclosed in a cage that slowly began to fall through the floor, descending into darkness until I landed at the bottom of a cave. I understood this cave to be my depression – that it existed in the pit of my soul, and it was where that gravitational pull originated from that I had been fighting against every day since.

That trip gave me an incredible gift though; while I was in the memory, I was able to pause and stretch out the moment before I walked into my house to face the aftermath of what I had just revealed. I saw myself sitting in this triangle of space suspended in time, drawing strength from this beautiful purple light that surrounded me. I was able to sit there and breathe, as long as I needed. It magically gave me a chance to embrace the small break between Mitch holding up the great burden I had just unloaded, and before the aftermath of despair and disruption had set in within my family and community.

The next trip came a few weeks later after I visited my parents' house and thought for the first time in over 20 years that I should look for the police report I had written when I was 16. I had this strong desire to find it, like it was the key to opening up the next level of healing for me. I found an entire file with my police report, a letter from the abuser to my family, and all the court and legal papers my parents had kept. I felt good about having the file with me, but opening it set my whole body into terrible anxiety and emotional flashbacks. I had no idea how I would ever read it without completely coming undone. I had tried a few times to flip through the papers and ended up needing multiple therapy sessions to help put myself back together after feeling like I had broken into a million pieces.

I had gone into my next planned trip day open to wherever my mind and the plant medicine wanted to take me. During this trip, I found myself inside my cave which had become a familiar place in my mind, but this time I was not alone. I experienced seeing myself at all different stages of my life, all hanging out together in my cave. Some were holding my little self as a baby and playing with the toddler me, my teenage self was there, and I saw older ones too. I saw all the way to my dying, old woman self, surrounded by some of the others. And with them all around me, I knew it was time to open up the file and read the 8-page police report I had somehow had the courage to write at 16 years old.

I came out of that experience feeling like I had written that report back then for me now in the present so that I could remember what had happened and finally free her from the cage she had been locked in all this time. It was such a life-changing experience, solidifying within me a sense of self and wholeness that had been missing from my life.

A few weeks later I was blessed with a psilocybin trip that felt like the bookend of that life experience. This time I was dancing in the forest, and the various ages of myself that I had seen previously had all come out to be with me. We were then joined by a host of other women; they were surrounding me and I was slowly spinning and reaching out, touching their hands and feeling their strength and power transfer to me. At that moment I felt that I was being given a gift from my ancestors and all the women before me, and understood that someday I would be on the other side, giving strength and power to other women in my current position.

This life-changing moment showed me that I was part of something greater and that I was not alone. Feeling the pull to check on that 16-year-old part of me, I opened up the file again. This time it was the letter from the abuser that came out. I had no idea what this letter would say, and until that moment I was unsure if I would ever be able to or even want to read it. But with all my selves and ancestors behind me, I felt strong and secure. I read the letter, which had been a genuine apology written to my family. I was transported in my mind to a blank open space where I saw my 16-year-old self to the left, and the former youth pastor to my right. I saw his pain and brokenness and how he had gotten off his path, and I saw that pain radiating from him and hitting the 16-year-old me. I was able to fully release him by severing the ropes that connected us, which stopped the ripple effect of pain and essentially freed my younger self from any ties to him. I came out of this vision believing that I had fully released him and the effects that situation had had on my life.

A few busy months passed, and I experienced two less satisfying trips. They came after an extremely challenging month, and in those times I found my emotions swirling around me like a hurricane. I couldn't latch on to anything and felt a little shaken up by them. Where were the beautiful trips that I had experienced so much healing from? Was any of it even real? I look back on those times now differently though. I had gotten away from my center, and had let family and school and life stress overtake me. I went into those trips thinking it would put me back together but instead it just shook everything up that had been swirling around in there anyway. I was able to release all that pent-up emotion and after getting the strength to try again, I was given the most beautiful gift from the mushrooms: a chance to meet and talk with my Higher Self.

After finally feeling like I had gotten my feet on solid ground again, I decided to try another mushroom trip. This time I went in with very few expectations, writing in my journal, "Choosing to really let go today and witness what comes. I'm not going to attach to anything, I'm going to try and just let it flow. Famous last words, right?" While listening to a guided meditation, my mind led me back to my cave, only this time my Higher Self was sitting at a little table waiting for me to join her. Her presence gave me a sense of security and warmth. I desperately wanted to see every detail of her, but she was blurry.

I sat down at the table, anxiously waiting for what was to unfold. She showed me that through the work I've done, my younger child self and my 16-year-old self were with her now, safe and wrapped in golden light. She then told me that I needed to go and collect my 17-year-old self, and in my mind, I was instantly transported to the scene of my car accident. I saw her sitting there in the snow with the smoking wreckage behind her, and I burst into tears as I realized that she had been frozen in that spot all this time. I heard my Higher Self say, "Thaw the snow; make it spring."

I saw snow and ice begin to melt as if we were in a time lapse of winter turning to spring. I saw flowers and mushrooms grow and pop up in and around the car that had been split in two from the accident. As I watched this unfold, I realized that time had caught up to the present and my 17-year-old self now looked completely different. I had been able to unfreeze her and change the smoking wreckage and snowy landscape into a beautiful garden full of life where she had been peacefully existing all this time; what a gift from that one mushroom trip.

This journey has brought me a freedom that I didn't realize was even possible, especially in such a short timeframe. I believe the psilocybin helped me rise above my pain, allowing my inner healer to take over and bring me through this journey of release. I hope my story can show others that healing is possible and that the gift of this plant medicine is life-changing and worth following if you hear it calling to you.

I am at the beginning of a new spiritual path and my mind has been opened to a whole world of possibilities. I can't even imagine what might come next!

Oh, and my depression is totally gone.

About The Author

My name is Jamie Church. I am an American living in Canada with my husband, our three kids, and a dog. I'm in grad school to become a therapist and hope to work in the field of Psychedelic Assisted Therapy so that I can help guide others on this amazing journey of awakening and listening to our inner healer. We have an entire universe of beauty and connectedness within us, and I hope that sharing some of my story will show readers how Sacred Plant Medicine is one of the many ways we can bring healing to past trauma and depression.

Feel free to connect with me at jamie.church@gmail.com

Psilocybin Mushrooms

Psilocybin mushrooms, also known as magic mushrooms, have been used for centuries in traditional indigenous practices for their spiritual and medicinal properties. In recent years, they have gained popularity among certain communities in the West for their psychedelic effects and potential for personal growth and spiritual exploration.

The use of psilocybin mushrooms can be approached in different ways, depending on the intention of the user and the cultural context in which they are used. In traditional indigenous practices, psilocybin mushrooms are often used in ceremonial settings, such as healing ceremonies or shamanic rituals. These ceremonies may involve singing, dancing, and other forms of prayer or meditation, and are typically led by an experienced shaman or healer.

In a modern context, psilocybin mushrooms are often used for recreational purposes or as a tool for personal growth and spiritual exploration. Many people choose to take psilocybin mushrooms in a safe and controlled setting, such as at home or in nature, with a trusted guide or friend. The experience may involve listening to music, engaging in introspective activities like journaling or meditation, or simply relaxing and enjoying the effects of the mushroom.

The effects of psilocybin mushrooms can vary depending on the dosage, the user's mindset and environment, and other factors. Typically, the effects of psilocybin mushrooms begin within 20-60 minutes of ingestion and can last for several hours. Some of the reported effects of psilocybin mushrooms include:

Altered perception of time and space

Visual and auditory hallucinations

Intense emotional experiences, both positive and negative
Increased creativity and openness
Spiritual or mystical experiences

It is important to note that the use of psilocybin mushrooms can be risky and potentially dangerous, especially if used without proper preparation and guidance from an experienced practitioner. Some of the reported risks associated with the use of psilocybin mushrooms include psychological distress, paranoia, and the potential for accidents or risky behavior while under the influence of the drug. Additionally, the use of psilocybin mushrooms is illegal in many countries, and possession or distribution of the mushrooms can result in serious legal consequences.

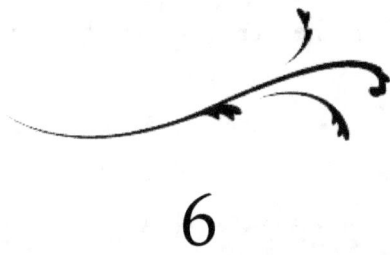

6

Tests, Allies & Enemies

I n the Hero's Journey, the phase of encountering tests, allies, and enemies is a crucial part of the hero's transformational journey. During this phase, the hero faces a series of challenges and obstacles that test their skills, knowledge, and courage. They also encounter allies who support them on their journey, as well as enemies who seek to thwart their progress.

Similarly, when we take psychedelics or enter shamanic ceremonies, we can also encounter a range of experiences that can be challenging, supportive, or obstructive. During an altered state of consciousness, we may encounter aspects of ourselves that we find difficult to face, such as unresolved emotions or fears. We may also encounter entities or spirits that can be either supportive or hostile.

Psychedelic and shamanic journeys can lead to a heightened sensitivity to one's surroundings, both internally and externally. In this state, we may confront inner challenges and obstacles, such as facing doubt or confronting past traumas. We may also encounter external allies, such as the shaman or other participants in the ceremony, who can offer guidance and support on their journey.

And we may also encounter perceived enemies, such as inner demons or negative thought patterns, that they must confront and overcome.

Just as the hero in the Hero's Journey must use their skills and knowledge to overcome obstacles and challenges, those taking psychedelics or entering shamanic ceremonies must also draw upon their inner resources to navigate their experience. This can involve developing a heightened sense of self-awareness and mindfulness, as well as learning how to surrender to the experience and trust the process.

In both cases, the encountering of tests, allies, and enemies can lead to personal growth and transformation. By facing challenges and obstacles, the hero in the Hero's Journey gains wisdom and experience that helps them on their journey. Similarly, by facing and integrating challenging aspects of ourselves during altered states of consciousness, we can gain a deeper understanding of ourselves and the world around us, and become more compassionate and empathetic towards others.

The encountering of tests, allies, and enemies can be intense and challenging, and individuals should take care to create a safe and supportive environment for their experience. It's important to note that taking psychedelics or entering shamanic ceremonies can vary widely depending on the individual, their set and setting, and other factors. It's crucial to approach these experiences with caution and respect, and to seek out experienced practitioners who can offer guidance and support on the journey.

You'll find an extensive list of preparation tips in the *Appendix* of this book.

The first story in this chapter by Julia Melville and Julia Coulson brings to light how dangerous the path of psychedelic healing can be. The two Julias want to lovingly ensure that people serving or taking sacred medicine know and trust the source of the medicine. They also warn how it's vital to know the practitioners are trustworthy. They relate some terrifying experiences they had with an unsavory practitioner and his medicine that we can all learn from.

How Well Do You Know Your Source?
By Julia Squared

We're here to share our experience with anyone working with the phenomenal healing properties of psychedelics, whether they are serving or receiving medicines. Our purpose is to highlight the importance of where medicines are sourced and the energy of the person who is serving the medicine.

The energy of the people who source or grow the medicine will be partially infused into the energy within the medicine. We want you to ask questions before deciding on who to work with. It is essential that the person serving the medicine has worked on their shadow side because their energy will also be served along with the medicine.

It is imperative to find out who has supplied the medicine to the practitioner, as well as examine the energy of the practitioner serving it to you. It is also vital to learn about the practitioner's relationship with the medicine and how long they have worked with it.

We are Julia Coulson and Julia Melville and together we run Julia2.com. We are both trained psychotherapists and have been working in this field for over 15 years. Our drive is to support people in understanding and connecting their relationship with self and how to regulate emotions. We believe that when we learn to regulate our own emotions, we don't always need anti-depressants or other medications.

About seven years ago, we felt a calling. It whispered the message that there was something able to take you deeper than talking therapy could reach. That was when our journeys with psychedelics began. Today, we have a lot of experience with many different medicines, both serving and receiving them.

We have always spoken about holding them sacredly in ceremony, knowing the source of the medicine and the energy of the person who is serving the medicine. We both learn experientially and found ourselves walking our talk when we recently traveled abroad for a Bufo facilitator training. Bufo is the common name given to the secretion from the Bufo Alvarius toad.

Bufo contains naturally occurring 5-MeO/DMT which is a powerful psychedelic compound. It helps us work through and release trauma held in the body through deep emotional release.

Red flags abound

Wisdom comes with hindsight. There was a riot of red flags that we had unintentionally ignored before going to this training. You might wonder why we ignored them, but in our experience with our many Kundalini Yoga trainings, there was always chaos before the training began. We thought the same thing was going on.

We had worked with Bufo for three years leading up to that point and asked people we knew about trainings, but no one knew of any. We resorted to searching on Google, and we came across what sounded like a really thorough training and just what we were looking for.

Based on the information we saw online, we liked their method of working and their ethos. We had a Zoom call with two out of the three facilitators and many text messages in between. We were put in touch with a WhatsApp group for recommendations on them. Interestingly, only 1 out of 5 people answered us.

The red flags kept coming. Three people independently told us to be very careful before leaving, as their intuition had rung alarm bells around the trip, and they didn't know why. We both had dreams that something wasn't right. When we went to pay for the training with the link that was sent to us, it went to a completely different person's name. When we questioned this, it was made light of. Our bank, even though we gave permission, still refused to pay them. The facilitators were angry at the bank questioning them. Yet we still went ahead!

On arrival at the venue, we settled in sitting and chatting to a couple of other people already there. The main facilitator, for this purpose we will call him Jon, received new medicine for the training and told us he always made sure it was 'clean' and good to use. He proceeded to smoke three pipes one after the other.

It made sense that he'd want to make sure the medicine was clean, but he smoked surprisingly large doses. It was at this point that we felt something wasn't in alignment with the way Jon reacted when he was on the medicine. He walked around looking at us in strange ways. It was creepy and scary.

On reflection, he was getting into our energy fields, spell casting. Later, he would tell us things about ourselves, a bit like a psychic does.

We started what was called the 'purification week' the following morning with a microdose of Bufo. We were surprised that there was no opening of the ceremonial space. We weren't smudged with sacred herbs or resins to cleanse and purify the ceremonial space or people, and no prayer or blessing was offered. This was very different from the many ceremonies we had previously with medicines. Bizarrely, it never occurred to us to question any of this, which could be called naive, but it also felt like there was an energetic seduction at play.

The microdose amount he served us was way above anything we were used to. No medicine was weighed, and we were often being served three pipes each time. We were familiar with weighed dosages but when we asked, we were told that it was all measured on intuition. This was the start of spiraling down into a very dark and unsafe space that was not emotionally held. We needed to feel safe for emotions to surface and be met with compassion and understanding, so that any vulnerability could be held in a grounded way.

The facilitators smoked pipes regularly outside of sessions and behaved strangely. We felt unsafe with no-one present emotionally and mentally to hold our internal space if confronting challenging emotions, memories and experiences emerged with the medicine. Holding space to us is an essential part of psychedelic experiences and is like being held in a safe bubble, unconditionally without judgment.

Kambo after bufo is a no-no

We were served Kambo for three days in a row, compulsory for this training. Kambo is a traditional Amazonian medicine and comes from the secretion of the Giant Green Monkey Tree Frog. Its scientific name is Phyllomedusa Bi-Color. Kambo is not psychedelic. It is a secretion full of peptides that include antibacterial, anti-microbial, anti-inflammatory and anti-depressant effects.

Kambo also contains many bioactive peptides, so when it enters the body, the cell receptors open and allow it to enter, to clean deposits left by foreign substances the cell was not able to process alone. Kambo also releases panema (negative energy) from the body. It offers immense benefits.

Kambo is a familiar medicine to us as we are both Kambo practitioners and know it is a strong caution not to receive Kambo immediately after Bufo as it can potentially trigger a psychotic experience. Even though we know this and advise this, somehow it just didn't occur to us.

The afternoons consisted of a 'main' Bufo session with a 'full' dosage. We expected to be held sacredly in a ceremonial space but again no opening prayer or smudging occurred. We were immediately served large amounts of Bufo. There was no difference in the amount of medicine used between the micro-dose and main sessions. Jon constantly smoked pipes during all sessions. He described himself as 'working' with people's energy fields.

One occasion, Jon fell to the ground after smoking a pipe that burned Julia M's ear. Another person was burned on their chest. Julia C had bruises down her legs and arms with a big bruise on the chin. She asked if she had banged her chin during a session and was told no. Another person fell backwards after being served Bufo, severely banging their head on a concrete floor. They were not attended to.

After the first full day we started to experience night terrors and have slightly divergent experiences. We have written our separate accounts below.

JULIA C

Before the first morning's 'micro-dose' was the last time I felt 'sober and grounded' that week. I was served so much medicine.

108

With every Bufo session I was catapulted into an utterly terrifying dark place. I never felt emotions were shifting, releasing or insightful like I had before with Bufo. Jon said the darkness was in me and my fault. He said I was a witch and needed to give up my black witch ways and that I hid from him in the medicine. He said every session I went into hell, he came and 'saved' me to bring me back. I was confused and didn't understand. This was unusual shadow work.

Jon said I was 'powerful' and put me on a 'no wants' diet. I wasn't allowed to want anything. I was to be in service to others, not thinking about myself. Any food I ate was to be given to me by others if they remembered, which is a tough ask when people are in their own process. I continued helping myself to drinking water and wondered if he wanted to completely break my spirit.

I stayed in a room with Julia after the first night. I didn't sleep the whole week. Every time I almost fell asleep, I felt myself fall into hell. Lost souls energetically around me lining up to be released through me, back to the light. Gray and white looking haggard and aged, thousands of them.

At different times during the night my body jolted as a malevolent spirit entered my body. It felt like my soul was sucked out of my body as these dark spirits wanted my body to have a 'form'. The energy felt evil and terrifying, and Jon's remedy was to serve me more Bufo to release them. In between these hellish experiences I got through nights listening to beautiful mantra music, repeating mantras to keep fear at bay.

I felt in a drugged state the whole time. My energy field was blasted open, and I didn't know what was real or not anymore. I lost myself and I lost my mind.

109

I became confused and paranoid. Voices in my head with no words and loud noises similar to the static of a television brought terrified agitation. I would cover my ears as though to stop hearing and scream, 'STOP'.

I carried a fleece blanket with me for comfort. I felt like a terrified child, terrified to be alone.

I experienced an overwhelming, all-consuming paranoia of wanting to kill myself. A tiny part of my logical mind could observe what was happening, and I asked people to remove glass pipes as the urge to break one and slash my wrists was powerful. In the garden a hammock rope was hanging from a tree. I walked to it, compelled to put a loop in it and wrap it round my neck. Thankfully, someone came so I wasn't left alone.

After an intense dark night, I asked not to have Bufo during the day as we were having a 'ceremony' with Samadhi overnight. From what I read and been told, this medicine produces a beautiful experience of bliss and as I hadn't taken it before, I was hopeful. A day off Bufo was a welcomed relief.

I was served Syrian Rue seeds, an MAO inhibitor, mixed with water, ground with my teeth to swallow. I had an uneasy feeling being served this by Jon and his helper, as I could hear them whispering 'make sure she drinks it all'. After a while I felt calm and relaxed, which actually felt nice.

Then, we were served Samadhi, again, watched by both to ensure I drank it all. After a while my head felt like a helicopter propeller whirling, round and round, a loud constant noise brought mental agitation that was seriously disturbing and terrifying and continued through the night.

My body expelled some of the medicine by projectile vomiting. It felt horrific and far from bliss. I screamed that I had been poisoned and drugged. I felt shamed as Jon said he was bored by my story. He induced Julia to collude in ridiculing me, calling me a victim. I felt worthless and abused but I could finally see his manipulations.

The morning after the Samadhi, Jon overheard me saying I would never take Samadhi again. He informed me I would, twice more. I said 'never,' and that I wanted to go home. His disposition changed and he got angry, 'is this how you repay me? You are on a no wants diet and yet you want to go home'. He ordered Julia to serve me a pipe.

No, I was not receiving more Bufo. At this point I feared for my life. I refused.

That evening Jon went out for dinner and energy at the center calmed. I went to bed feeling calm. A few hours later when he returned, so did the negative energies and dark spirits. In that sober moment I connected to an inner knowing that said get the hell out of there.

I spent six weeks physically recovering after returning home with chronic diarrhoea and nausea. My body craved fruits and vegetables. Everything I ate went straight through me. I became sensitive to any chemical smells and could taste chemicals in tap water that made me nauseous.

Mentally I had no energy or concentration for conversation. I was terrified to be alone and slept with the light on. The night terrors slowly subsided after four weeks. Energetically, it took over four months to recover and feel whole again.

JULIA M

On our first full day I received the news from home that my darling mother-in-law had suffered a bad stroke. I wanted to go home but was reassured by my family to stay and we would keep in touch. I know in my heart that this happened to bring me home. I felt very far from home and not totally supported and safe, but I pushed these feelings to the back of my mind.

On our second night after our full day of training, and every night following before returning home, I had dark night terrors. I became scared to go to bed as I knew it would be similar to the night before. I felt confused because during the day I was reassured by Jon that everything was as it should be. But in the dark quiet hours it felt far from being OK.

On our third day I again said I wanted to go home because the training was not what I had expected and was too intense, and I didn't feel safe. I am still bemused as to why I accepted sitting with Kambo after Bufo when I knew that this wasn't a good practice. During my second Kambo ceremony I had the most intense experience I have ever had with what is usually a beautiful medicine. I had asked not to sit with Kambo for the required three times but again was reassured that it was necessary for the purification process.

On Day 4 I talked again about going home. I was feeling out of my depth and disorientated. The lack of sleep was wearing me out and the dark energies that came through at night were getting more powerful. I found myself releasing many, many lost souls from the First and Second World Wars, information coming through about a family member who was unwell, and releasing dark energy from around them. The medicine evoked the most powerful energies I have experienced, and my body would shake uncontrollably.

I was also scared by how Julia was behaving, in a way I had never seen before. Again, I was reassured that it was all as it was meant to be and told that it was normal that she would become paranoid. I accepted this at the time but looking back I wonder, what the hell was I thinking?

On our fifth day we had an evening ceremony with the medicine, Samadhi. We were told it was the medicine of light. It was not a medicine I was familiar with, so I didn't know what to expect. We were served an MAO inhibitor of Syrian Rue seeds prior to the Samdhi which helped to relax us and it felt a very gentle altered state to be in. We waited for about half an hour and then were served the Samadhi. Almost instantly, I was thrown into hell and anyone who has been there will understand what I am saying.

I have never seen black look so black, with terrifying dark energies trying to wrap themselves around me. I endured projectile vomiting and sheer terror. After I don't know how long, I became aware of lying beneath some shutters where there was a sliver of light above my head and in front of me up on the wall was a painting of what looked like Christ's hand reaching out. When I kept my eyes open and stayed aligned with the light, I could fight the dark forces off. I connected with God, with Jesus and Archangel Michael — the purest energy which supported me in a way that words cannot express.

When we eventually got to bed the terrifying dark energies returned. The following day we were offered more medicine which I refused. I wasn't in a strong enough space to have any medicine as I was feeling saturated on a physical and emotional level. I felt toxic inside rather than clear and light.

One of our colleagues left as he was in a place of severe disorientation.

That night in the early hours Julia said we needed to leave immediately. We spent the next few hours changing our flights, packing and making arrangements to leave, so that we couldn't be deterred or have anyone convince us we needed to stay.

I continued to have night terrors for two weeks after returning home and couldn't go into dark rooms on my own. I had to sleep holding onto my husband as I didn't feel safe. With a massive amount of energy work, support and calling in Higher energies, this thankfully dissipated over the following weeks.

Moving forward

As we reflect on this story, we can't believe how hoodwinked and seduced we became in accepting how we were being treated. We believed his talk. His intentions and words were good, but his actions were dangerous.

When ceremonies are not held safely, it opens gateways to very dark energies to come into energy fields. These dark energies are around us all the time, and that is why it is so important that space is honored sacredly in ceremony and ritual with divine love. We now have a greater understanding of holding space in a stronger way than before.

We are so grateful to be here to tell our story. We don't regret this experience as we have learnt so much and have a deeper respect for these powerful medicines that can release trauma or handled incorrectly, create trauma. We both believe everything happens for a reason, and clearly we needed to have this experience to help us grow as practitioners. Know the source of any medicine you receive.

About The Authors

Julia Melville is an Accredited Psychotherapist, Kundalini Yoga Teacher, Kambo Practitioner and Medicine Woman. Through her practice with 1:1 work, retreats and ceremonies, she supports people in understanding their relationship with their own energies and how they impact us physically, mentally, emotionally, and spiritually.

Having grown up with periods of binge eating, bulimia, drugs, alcohol, over-exercising and a dialogue of inner criticism, Julia's work is driven by knowing that through changing self-sabotaging behavior and the negative stories that we tell ourselves, it is possible to have a more compassionate and loving relationship with self. Working with the combination of plant medicines and psychotherapy has helped Julia to find stillness and harmony within. Gratitude for this process and all it has given her is at the heart of what drives her to share it with others.

Julia is married and has three daughters. She lives with her husband, three dogs and two tortoises.

Julia Coulson is a Psychotherapist with an interest in psychedelics and plant medicines, Supervisor, Kundalini Yoga teacher, Kambo practitioner, Mystic and Wild Medicine woman running retreats and ceremonies.

She has traveled and worked with tribes in Peru, Mexico and Colombia using different Psychedelics and plant medicines. She has worked in Connecticut with people impacted by trauma from the Sandy Hook shooting, and trainings have taken her around the world, including Europe, India and USA.

Julia grew up in a dysfunctional family experiencing emotional abuse, sexual abuse, and death of a parent as a baby, with anorexia and suicide attempts as a teenager.

Julia is passionate about her work and wants to help people discover the truth of who they are under their trauma. Believing trauma doesn't have to define who we are, Julia knows change is possible - to feel free, comfortable in our own skin and to love the life we live from our hearts.

Julia and Julia co-run a Wellness Centre. Please visit www.Julia2.com

Beware of the rent-a-shaman

Based on the previous story, I want to call attention to the emergence of what I call the 'rent-a-shaman'. Even in South America, you can find folks willing to serve you the powerful ayahuasca brew at the same place you buy bubble gum and altitude sickness pills. In New York City, you could attend an ayahuasca gathering with someone who sat in a few ceremonies and felt called to serve the medicine without any direct lineage initiation.

The process of becoming a shaman in indigenous cultures varies depending on the specific traditions and beliefs of the community. However, there are some general patterns that are often seen across different cultures.

Indigenous people who become shamans often undergo a rigorous and transformative process that involves personal growth, spiritual exploration, and community support.

In many cultures, becoming a shaman involves a calling or vision. This can occur through a dream, an illness, or an encounter with a spirit or otherworldly entity that signal a special connection to the spiritual realm. This calling may be confirmed by other members of the community who recognize the person's potential as a healer or spiritual leader.

Once the calling is established and accepted, the person may undergo a period of isolation or training to learn the skills and knowledge necessary to become a shaman. The individual will also become an apprentice with an experienced shaman, during which they learn the necessary skills and knowledge to fulfill their role.

This training may involve learning about herbal medicine, ritual practices, and the use of trance states to communicate with spirits or ancestors. The apprentice may also undergo a period of purification or initiation, which can involve fasting, isolation, or other challenging experiences. These rituals are designed to help the person develop a deeper connection to the spiritual realm and to prepare them for their role as a shaman.

In some cultures, becoming a shaman may also involve a hereditary component, with certain families or lineages having a tradition of shamanism that is passed down through generations. In these cases, the individual may still undergo a period of training and initiation to fully develop their abilities.

After completing their training, the person may begin to serve their community as a shaman. This may involve performing healing ceremonies, providing spiritual guidance, and leading ritual ceremonies. The shaman may also continue to develop their skills and knowledge throughout their lifetime through ongoing training and spiritual practice.

Overall, becoming a shaman in indigenous cultures is often seen as a spiritual calling that involves a deep connection to the natural world, the spirit realm, and the community. It requires a combination of innate talent, dedication, and training to become a respected and effective shaman. The shamanic training path is a complex and multifaceted process that involves a deep connection to spirituality, a commitment to personal growth, and a strong connection to cultural traditions.

Kambo

Kambo, also known as Sapo, is a traditional Amazonian medicine made from the secretions of the Phyllomedusa bicolor frog. The frog is not harmed during the collection process, which involves gently scraping the secretion from the frog's skin and releasing it back into the wild.

The secretion contains a complex mixture of bioactive peptides, including several peptides with potent pharmacological properties. When kambo is applied to the skin, usually by burning small holes in the skin and applying the secretion to the wounds, the peptides can enter the bloodstream and produce a range of effects.

Kambo has been used for centuries by indigenous tribes in the Amazon region for a variety of purposes, including as a medicine for physical and emotional ailments, as well as for hunting and other ceremonial purposes. Some of the reported benefits of kambo include:

Boosting the immune system: Kambo has been shown to stimulate the immune system, increasing the production of white blood cells and other immune cells.

Detoxification: Kambo has been reported to have detoxifying effects, helping to eliminate toxins from the body and promote overall health.

Pain relief: Kambo has been used to alleviate pain, including chronic pain and headaches.

Emotional healing: Kambo is believed to have psychological and emotional healing properties, helping to alleviate symptoms of anxiety, depression, and PTSD.

It is important to note that kambo can be a powerful medicine with potentially serious risks and side effects. The use of kambo should only be done under the guidance of a trained practitioner in a safe and controlled setting. Additionally, kambo is illegal in some countries, and possession or distribution of the secretion can result in serious legal consequences.

Bufo

Bufo, also known as Bufo alvarius or the Colorado River toad, is a species of toad that is found in the southwestern United States and northern Mexico. The toad is known for its powerful psychoactive properties, as its skin contains a potent hallucinogenic substance called 5-MeO-DMT.

5-MeO-DMT is a naturally occurring psychedelic compound that produces intense spiritual and mystical experiences when ingested. In traditional indigenous practices, the Bufo toad has been used in shamanic rituals for thousands of years to induce altered states of consciousness and facilitate spiritual transformation.

In recent years, the use of 5-MeO-DMT from the Bufo toad has gained popularity among certain communities in the West as a tool for personal growth and spiritual exploration. Advocates of the practice believe that the experience can provide insights into the nature of reality, the self, and the universe.

The most common way that Bufo, or Bufo alvarius toad venom, is taken is by smoking the dried venom. The venom is extracted from the toad's glands and then dried, usually on a piece of glass or other non-reactive surface. The dried venom is then scraped off and smoked in a pipe, vaporizer, or other smoking device.

In some cases, the dried venom may be mixed with other herbs or substances, such as tobacco or cannabis, to help facilitate the smoking process or enhance the experience. Another less common method of taking Bufo is through vaporization. This involves heating the dried venom to a high temperature, which produces a vapor that can be inhaled. Vaporization is considered to be a more efficient method of ingestion than smoking, as it allows for a higher concentration of the active compounds to be absorbed into the bloodstream.

There are also reports of Bufo being taken orally, either in the form of a tea or by swallowing the venom directly. However, this method is considered to be less effective than smoking or vaporization, as the active compounds in the venom are not easily absorbed by the digestive system.

It is important to note that the use of Bufo toad venom or 5-MeO-DMT can be risky and potentially dangerous, especially if used without proper preparation and guidance from an experienced practitioner. Some of the reported risks associated with the use of Bufo toad venom include respiratory distress, cardiac complications, and psychological distress. The use of Bufo toad venom is also illegal in many countries, and possession or distribution of the venom can result in serious legal consequences.

PART 3
TRANSFORMATION

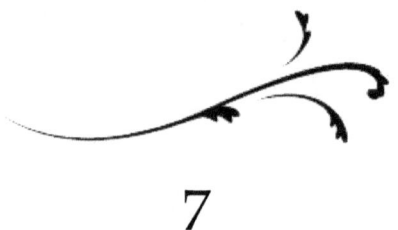

7

Approaching the Cave

Approaching the inmost cave is the first part of a critical transformation phase in the Hero's Journey of self-discovery. This phase represents a moment of deep introspection and reflection, where the hero must confront their deepest fears, doubts, and insecurities. The cave is often symbolized by an inner cave or labyrinth. This phase is a critical moment of self-reflection and reckoning, where the hero must prepare themselves for the ultimate ordeal ahead.

Similarly, taking psychedelics or entering shamanic rituals can be seen as a way of approaching the inmost cave. Once the medicine is in full effect, going deep within, beyond the normal waking reality, we can feel like we are becoming cocooned in darkness or lost in a cave. We may feel like we are on a journey towards the deepest parts of our psyche, where we will confront our most challenging inner demons. In these experiences of heightened self-awareness and introspection, we are often forced to confront our deepest fears, doubts, and insecurities. This can be a difficult and uncomfortable process, as it may involve reliving past traumas, confronting negative thought patterns, and facing the existential mysteries of life.

However, by entering into this state of deep introspection and reflection, individuals may be able to gain new insights and perspectives on themselves, their innermost desires, and their place in the world. It can be a transformative process, as individuals may be forced to see aspects of themselves that they have long repressed or denied. They may be able to confront and overcome their deepest fears and doubts, gaining a sense of inner strength and resilience. They may also gain a deeper understanding of the interconnectedness of all things and a greater appreciation for the mystery and beauty of existence. They will also explore their own identity.

It's important to note that approaching the inmost cave, whether through the Hero's Journey or through the use of psychedelics or shamanic rituals, is not without risks. The experience can be intense and overwhelming, and individuals may need to approach it with caution and with the guidance of experienced practitioners. However, for those who are able to navigate this phase of their journey and fully embrace or surrender to it, it can be a transformative and life-changing experience, allowing one to emerge with a greater sense of self-awareness, acceptance, and compassion.

Our first story in this chapter by Kate Church explore how the fear of going within can be met with healing and transformation. At first, Kate was afraid and mistrustful of the effects magic mushrooms would have on her. However, desperate to heal from PTSD and a debilitating autoimmune disease, she decided to give psilocybin a try. She found renewal and alignment, along with healing effects in body, mind, and soul.

Our second story by Irina Vlada, highlights how entering the cave through psychedelics may be the only way through the desperation and hopelessness we face. Irina lived in luxury and success yet hated her life. Despite appearing like a shining star to others, inside she was a mess of uppers and downers, eating disorders, compulsive spending, and toxic relationships. Her suicidal ideations inspired her to go to Columbia and try ayahuasca. Fortunately, she emerged with courage to live.

Sacred Surrender
By Kate Church

Microdosing mushrooms first appeared on my radar back in 2018. My friend started taking them for his anxiety and couldn't stop praising them for their magical effects (pun intended). He recommended them to me as I worked and lived in a high-stress environment. However, I wasn't ready to relinquish my sense of control to a psychedelic, which I mistakenly and ignorantly believed would cause me to hallucinate uncontrollably and potentially lose my mind. After all, the 1970s "war on drugs" had won and its message was still going strong three decades later due to steadfast media conditioning. I'd also been indoctrinated by my education system while growing up in the late 90s and early 2000s.

It wasn't until I watched the Netflix documentary, *Have a Good Trip*, in 2020 during the worldwide COVID-19 pandemic that I started seeing mushrooms and the psychedelic effects of their psilocybin as a potentially non-harmful substance. As the documentary was more entertainment-based than medical-based, I started to research psilocybin more, reading scholarly articles and case studies, listening to podcasts, and of course watching more documentaries, including *Fantastic Fungi*. As I delved into my research, I continuously read about, heard about, and saw the ability psilocybin had to resolve trauma and PTSD.

Resisting to rest

This avenue was of particular interest to me as I had been struggling with trauma and PTSD since the age of 4 (my first core memory). I'd been experiencing frequent night terrors, insomnia, paranoia, depression, anxiety, and panic attacks. Now, in 2020 at the age of 26, with an increasing number of traumatic experiences under my belt and hardwired into my brain, my fully formed prefrontal cortex and I were ready to heal.

However, that is always easier said than done. The task of healing is quite daunting and easy to dismiss, but highly necessary. Especially at this point in time as I had been diagnosed with an often debilitating autoimmune condition called myositis, where the immune system attacks muscles and breaks them down at an accelerated rate. During the diagnosis phase, I experienced increasingly painful muscle cramping and spasms, constant vertigo and tinnitus, temporary vision impairment, and immobility due to my muscles giving out.

There were days when I couldn't leave my bed because I couldn't stand. When I could stand and walk, there were days when I couldn't hold or open anything. When I could hold and open anything, my hands often cramped up around the object and there was no removing it without injury. I often would wake up with T-Rex arms, try to work with T-Rex arms, and go to bed with T-Rex arms. Some days I would wake up perfectly fine and feel healthy. I would go about my day and then suddenly a flare-up would ensue and I would be in shambles.

To make matters worse, none of the medications I'd been prescribed was working. When I went off my various immune system-suppressing medications, my doctor informed me that if the myositis went unchecked or untreated for too long, the "incurable" autoimmune condition could lead to my immune system attacking my organs. While the symptoms were very real, I refused to accept this prognosis, which is why I've put quotations around "incurable".

There are many incurable autoimmune conditions that are debilitating, life-altering and life-threatening, and I'd never want to demean or dismiss that, but I personally never want to accept that any illness or disability I wasn't born with isn't curable. Delusional? Possibly. Hopeful? Absolutely. What is the opposite of hope? Despair. And what causes despair? Stress. Which I had in ABUNDANCE.

"Stress kills". We've all heard that saying before, we've all dismissed that saying before, and sooner or later, we will all experience that saying either before or after it's too late. I was lucky enough to experience that saying before it was too late. That may be an odd thing to say as being diagnosed with an incurable and possibly deadly autoimmune condition isn't something one would consider lucky, but what can I say, I was in my new era of hope. After all, I understood what had triggered this autoimmune reaction.

My decades of trauma and PTSD were finally physically manifesting after my stressful and often predatory work environment triggered a chain reaction of nervous system overload, demanding that I finally come out of fight or flight and move into rest and recovery. And if there was any time to find the time to rest and recover, it was while the entire world went in and out of lockdown for the next two years.

During those two years, I found a lot of rest, but not a lot of recovery. I had put off using the sacred medicine yet again and was working with several autoimmune specialists who only took Western medicine into consideration. This resulted in my autoimmune condition getting worse, and every doctor either dismissing me or eventually giving up on me, with my primary doctor prescribing oxycontin for my pain. I refused the oxy, although it had been in my coping arsenal for over a decade.

I bawled my eyes out at the end of every appointment, trying to elicit any sort of sympathy from my different doctors, desperately wanting them to take another look and run another test, but those tears were to no avail. I was continuously left alone, angry and exhausted. How could those who are meant to heal, who took an oath to do no harm, not take either of those dedications seriously? Not only did those doctors waste my time, but they also wasted my resources and energy. Any blip of hope and health was gone.

A new approach

After my final specialist visit, I met up with my friend for lunch. Puffy-eyed from crying, I leaned on my friend, and wine, for support. We got drunk, which was not good for my health, but during that drunken lunch, which then turned into dinner, we decided to go to the John Mayor concert with a few friends that night. This was good for my health, as I am a firm believer that community and music have the power to heal on the deepest level. As my friends and I swayed to the music and spilled wine everywhere, psychedelic patterns filled John Mayor's backdrop. "I should try mushrooms". This thought was met with no resistance. Once the hangover had cleared the next day, the thought arose again. "I should try mushrooms." Again, this thought was met with no resistance. It was time.

I started with micro-dosing mushrooms for about three months. During that time, I experienced significant stress reduction and groundedness in my everyday life. I was able to get out of my head and into my body. My autoimmune condition and its symptoms improved significantly, with decreasing muscle cramps and spasms and relief from vertigo, tinnitus and any vision impairment, but I wasn't fully healed yet. I still struggled with severe flare-ups and the anxiety lessened, but was still present. After all, going from fully able to disabled in mere seconds is incredibly daunting. With that in mind, I slowly increased my dose with caution and slight hesitation lingering in the back of my mind, until one day I decided to take the plunge, desperate to overcome my fears and failing health. I had done the research, now it was time to do the work.

Mushrooms, medicine, and memories

Before taking the medicine, I sat with it and myself and set an intention. A broad intention of inviting in any healing that needed to happen, but an intention nonetheless. I set up my space, cleared the energy in the room with sage and smudging bells, and changed into comfortable clothing. Down the hatch went 2 grams of the medicine as I sat in meditation awaiting the healing to come. About an hour or so later it hit, and when I say it hit, it HIT. Zero to one hundred. Meditation to magic. Awareness to awakening.

To be honest, I was quite overwhelmed at first. It was such a drastic shift and my thoughts came rushing in without control. As an avid meditator, I thought I knew how to sit with myself, but it felt as if my psyche was fighting me. I couldn't make up my mind. I wanted to go outside and lie in the grass, I wanted to shower, I wanted to clean, I wanted to eat, I wanted to masturbate, I wanted to sleep. But nothing felt right because I wanted to do any sort of physical task that would take my attention away from the medicine

131

and away from sitting in stillness with myself, and that's not how it works.

I had no other option but to lean into it and try my best to enjoy the ride. After all, I'd set the broad intention of inviting in any healing that needed to happen, and it was time for me to do my part. I'd called on the medicine and now it was calling on me.

I took a deep breath and started grounding myself. I turned the lights off, put on a sound bath song called "Rebirth" which always brings me to ease, and lay down on the floor. As I listened to the music and melted into the floor, I decided I needed a release. I started to do the Tension and Trauma Release Exercise (TRE) created by Dr. David Bercelu. I started to cry. Doing this exercise was normal for me, but crying was not. I let the tears flow and my body shake. As I surrendered to the medicine and myself, I started seeing memories of abandonment.

There was a deep mother wound that I'd never known was present, as my father wound had always taken center stage. I continued to cry and shake as the memories made themselves known. As each memory rose, I would shake and cry harder. As each memory was released, I'd stop shaking and crying and start to laugh, feeling a deep sense of relief, joy, love, and oneness. I went on like this for what seemed to be an eternity but was probably only an hour or two. Once the mother wound had been fully realized and released, it was time to work on my general outlook on life. After all, I'd set a broad intention, so I was getting a broad spectrum of healing.

I started talking out loud as I lay on the floor in stillness. "I'm so bored, I'm so bored, I'm so bored". I started yelling at the universe. "I'm so bored, I'm so bored, I'm so bored!". I felt as if I was in a prison, or like an alien in a meatsuit it doesn't want to wear.

Trapped in body and in time. My yelling was then interrupted by uncontrollable yawning. I'm bored, I'm tired, I'm angry. In between yawning, I yelled, "This place is a prison, my body is a prison, time is a prison!". During the yawning, I heard, "Reality is relative; you create your own prison". My mind then went to the ocean, the place I feel most free and at ease. I started to cry and shake again.

Curled up in the fetal position, I heard, "You must learn to hold yourself in your grief before you can hold others". When the tears had stopped, I looked up and saw a strand of my hair hanging off of my desk chair. I thought, "This is all that will be left of me one day", and started to laugh uncontrollably. "This is so stupid, fears are so stupid, this is a joke, life is a joke and I pranked myself." I started to cry again.

"Healing hurts". I said this over and over again until the laughter came back. "Oh no", I said as I started to cry. "Okay cool", I said as I started to laugh. I went back and forth between dread and joy for over an hour. Experiencing and expressing two vital forms of healing. As the last of my tears fell, I wiped them away.

I then became obsessed with my hands. Still lying on the floor, but now facing upwards, I started to stare at the palms of my hands. In the palm of my left hand, I saw the face of a bear; in the palm of my right hand, I saw the face of a bunny. The longer I stared, the more the animals came to life. I was thoroughly intrigued. About a year prior I'd done a past life regression hypnosis. In this hypnosis, I'd been asked to have my spirit animal step forward. A bear and a bunny appeared. The same bear and bunny I now saw in the palm of each hand. "This wasn't in my daily horoscope", I said out loud. The laughter started up again, but the tears were tapped out. As I laughed, I started to feel at peace. Still staring at my hands, I was so confused, but I didn't care because it didn't matter. I was finally starting to enjoy the ride. Anything and everything was hilarious to me, and I didn't have a care in the world.

While starting to come down, I got off the floor and decided to burn Palo Santo. The lighter wouldn't work. "That's okay, I don't want to work either." The laughter came back as I thought to myself, "I'm a comedic show for one. Anything that comes my way I can laugh off." I felt lighter. I felt renewed. I felt aligned. I felt it was time for bed. After all, crying is an exhausting sport.

The next morning, I woke up feeling heavy. Covered in a cloud of emotion and exhaustion, I was reeling from the healing. Still processing the process. In hindsight, I shouldn't have taken the medicine on a Sunday, but I am still glad I did. Come Tuesday, the cloud was lifted and so was I.

Still on the path

As I continue to go back to the medicine, I find that my initial feelings of renewal and alignment have stayed with me, while I continue to dive deeper into my healing and myself. Each time I either increase or decrease my dose depending on my level of comfort while setting a new intention and experiencing a new form of healing. The medicine has a way of knowing what needs to be done, what needs to be healed and in what order. It's peeling the trauma back one layer at a time, but instead of peeling inwards, it peels outwards. Starting from the root and branching up.

I continue to be surprised by the medicine and its depth. The deeper I go, the higher I grow, shedding old traumas, stress paradigms, and unhealthy thought patterns and habits. In turn, healing my autoimmune condition, opening my heart and revealing my soul. These positive and sacred healing effects stay with me, and

I can go back to them continuously, surrendering to the sacred medicine as it lovingly shares its sacred healing with me.

About The Author

Kate Church is a freelance writer based in Toronto, Canada. She is interested in exploring art, culture, travel, and healing modalities.

She can be reached at katevchurch@gmail.com.

Courage to Live
By Irina Vlada

It was another early morning after a sleepless night in downtown New Orleans. The private entrance of the luxury condominium slowly opened, and I drove my pearl-white E-class Mercedes through the gate. My eyes were full of tears as I kept my shaking hands on the leather steering wheel. I anxiously counted the floors of the building in front of me. My balcony was on the 18th floor. 'Are 18 floors enough? What if it doesn't work?' I thought, frustrated. 'How can I get to the roof?'

'I hate who I am,' my thoughts continued. 'I am a total mistake in this life. I just want it to be over.' The feeling of unworthiness overtook my mind and body once again.

How did I end up here? What went wrong for a girl who'd moved to America at the age of 19 with only $200 in her pocket? Back then, I spoke no English and didn't know a soul in this foreign land. Yet, here I was, just a few years later, a business school graduate, making good money and keeping company with celebrities, NFL players, local politicians and business owners. To the outside world, I was shining like a star at every public event, perfectly presented and glowing. But I looked through completely empty eyes, sharing fake smiles and superficial conversations, and at the heart of it all, living with addiction.

At the time that I was contemplating suicide, I was relying on amphetamines in the morning and downers at night. I also struggled with eating disorders, compulsive consumption, and toxic relationships. My addictions to negativity, consumption, control, and escapism all stemmed from my trauma and emotional pain. I was looking for any way to leave behind shame, regret and self-pity.

Sitting there in my car, tears streaming down my face, my soul felt lonely. I was lost. Yet, despite paralysing fear in my body, courage was present in my heart. "What would it take to jump? Courage," I thought. "And what will it take to live? Courage."

That painful moment was a gift and an opportunity to choose change. In my longing for physical death, I'd unearthed a fundamental truth: it was a spiritual death that I was truly seeking. I could be born anew into the person I was ready to become. I was ready to die, and therefore transform, grow, and blossom.

It is fascinating how an encounter with death can bring us closer to life. In a split second, I became curious about what it means to be alive. What matters in life the most? I couldn't answer, yet I took my eyes off the building in front of me and gently closed my eyelids. My mind was anxiously looking for a solution, a sign, guidance, or words of wisdom: rehab, retreat, therapist, psychiatrist, coach, shaman, ayahuasca... ayahuasca. Ayahuasca.

I turned off the car and chose to jump inward.

Courage to change

Six months later, I was sitting under the stars in Colombia, accepting my first cup of ayahuasca from a shaman.

The initial sip took me straight to a colourful labyrinth. I experienced fast-paced movement down infinite rainbow corridors. Slightly nauseated from all the internal dynamics, I opened my eyes and found that my physical reality was blurry. I tried to get up a few times, but my out-of-balance body was quickly pulled back to my blanket.

The shaman noticed my attempt to move and walked towards me. 'How are you feeling?' he asked in Spanish. I do not speak his language, yet could feel what his words meant. 'I'm stuck in the bubble gum room and I have no desire to be here,' I mumbled. He nodded his head like he knew my exact location then walked away to return with my second cup.

People often ask, how many cups should you have during an ayahuasca ceremony? After many ceremonies with the Colombian tribe, I've realised that it's an individual call. Trust your intuition and your shaman's recommendations.

After my second cup, I experienced existence to the fullest. I envisioned the turquoise spiral at my third eye with endless numbers of eyes and peacock feathers. Observing the inner spiral gave me an immediate blissful experience. The spiral and my awareness journey towards its centre were eternal.

When my attention was distracted by doubts or fears, and I would lose the perception of bright colours and vibration changed to dissonance, all I had to do was repeat 'ayahuasca' in my consciousness. Like a secret code, my attention would shoot straight back into the ecstasy-like feeling.

In hindsight, the ceremony was a profound experience in learning the 'power of my own attention'. The old phrase, 'Where our attention goes, energy flows,' is correct. When we learn to consciously choose the object of our attention, we begin to train and strengthen the most powerful and yet least tangible muscle of our being – our attention. Remember: our power is based on the choices we make to evoke courage and ultimately create change.

As the experience continued, I found myself observing the wheel of life, samsara, turning and spinning, exposing to me the whole history of humanity. I witnessed the pyramids of Giza emerging out of nowhere and dissolving back into the desert sands. I saw our most significant spiritual masters walking the earth, and I even saw myself as them. The circle began to spin so fast that I simply got tired of following it. It made me slightly nauseous. I purged.

Once again, back in my body, I felt dissociated and confused, like when waking up from a vivid dream. Everything around me felt scary. People were making noises reminiscent of a psychiatric hospital and periodically purging on my left and right. There were about twenty of us, each curled on our blankets under the night sky. Fear and judgement surged through me. I was disgusted by what I observed through blurry vision. Why am I here? What kind of substance is this? Who are these people? What would my parents say? What is the shaman?... and I purged again. Looking back, I realise that I was purging judgement, fear, and shame.

The last thing I remember from the experience was becoming an embryo in my mother's womb. I witnessed my development through different stages, and felt the sound of her heartbeat. It sounded like I was under water. I physically felt the spinning and turning of "coming back to life". I travelled between being inside my mother in a pre-birth state and being on the ground with my hands grasping at the soil, grass, or anything I could lay my hands on to feel alive, to survive, to exist.

When I finally re-entered physical reality, everyone else had disappeared. I felt joy, without understanding where the joy was coming from. Was I happy to return? Was I happy to be alive? Did I die at all? Or did I simply dream about everything and nothing at all? For the first time in my life, I experienced true gratitude for existence itself.

Courage to fail

Ayahuasca was an intense experience. My expectation had been that it would fix me, make me whole and give me answers. Yet here I was, more confused than ever before. My gratitude for life faded rapidly, leaving me with heightened self-awareness and more fear than I could process. The feeling of loneliness increased. I felt anxious to meet with people I used to call friends. Public places made me feel suspicious, judged, and afraid. I spent more time at home, reading books on self-healing and trying to overcome my ego.

Yet Ayahuasca did heal something. It annihilated my addictions at the root! There was no longer a sign of any longing for amphetamines, downers or unhealthy food consumption. Yet, I was overwhelmed with anxiety, low self-esteem, lethargic energy, and gut issues. The chemicals that I had taken for years coupled with my eating disorder had harmed my digestive system. I had a long journey ahead of me to heal physically and emotionally, and it took a last drop of courage to continue forward.

Change can sound exciting, and even sexy. But sometimes it looks like quitting your job, taking a semester off, gaining weight, sleeping till 12 pm and having a bloated stomach. Instead of feeling like I'd won, I felt like I'd lost everything. I lost my outer beauty and inner fire. I had to let go of my illusionary fame and connections because I had zero desire or tolerance to be in public, which deepened my feeling of unworthiness and loneliness. I was in need of further healing. My emotional well-being became my priority, and it inspired my commitment to real and sustainable change – conscious change.

There is a great responsibility that comes with a psychedelic medicine experience. With the expansion of your self-awareness, you can no longer blame anyone else for the situation in your external world, and your victimhood dies. You realise that change starts from within. It evokes a radical self-responsibility and strengthens the inner power.

Courage to try again

The sun was coming up in the morning sky, exposing a majestic view of the Himalayan mountains. Meditating by the Ganges River was our daily practice at Sattva Yoga Academy. It was my second month of living in India and studying yoga: chanting mantras, practising breathwork and kriya, eating vegetarian meals, and listening to the source of wisdom through my guru, Anand Mehrotra.

Through yoga, I've learned that our true purpose in life is to evolve, to expand our consciousness beyond the limiting stories of the mind, to serve others on our path, and to cultivate gratitude and reverence towards life. Yogic techniques support the evolution of our consciousness where we align our physical body, refine the nervous system, and clarify the mind with correct knowledge. The unity that yoga stands for is the unity within us, the coherence of our heart and mind.

I've experienced altered states of consciousness through powerful breathwork and kriya movement in the many hours of practice with my teacher. I've seen the same spiral in the mind's eye through the pranayama techniques as I did through psychedelic medicine. It is possible to achieve an expanded awareness of self with only your mind, body and spirit. These methods strengthen the nervous system and prepare the mind for our return to the physical body in a gentle way, where there is less intensity or confusion.

Certainly, psychedelic medicine can be a powerful tool, a breakthrough for a stagnant state of consciousness that would be difficult to achieve through yogic practice. It is important to realise that psychedelics are not magic pills, and there are no shortcuts in life. The true power lies in our prepared nervous system and ability to integrate any life experience.

Coming back to 'normal' life after being in India was similar to returning to the 'real' world from a psychedelic experience. Intense. Unknown. Frightening. Slightly confusing. My self-awareness and the insights that I'd gained from the healing journey were my greatest tool. Healing is not a destination; it is a journey, a curvy path towards self-love.

Practising yoga and honouring my self-awareness create a loving path towards my inner healing. Yoga encourages me to be compassionate towards myself, to accept past choices, and to move forward by applying new knowledge and insights. It is a lifelong practice – to accept the unacceptable, to forgive the unforgivable, to love the unlovable, and therefore to be whole.

Courage to be yourself

I put the velvet eye mask on my face, pulled a soft wool blanket over my body, and started to relax into the sound of the binaural beats. My awareness began to drift away as the ketamine took hold. I felt like I was physically floating, present yet distant, in my own bedroom. Breathing slowly and steadily, I observed my thoughts and feelings without judgement.

Psychedelic medicine is a journey inward. It can be as gentle or as intense as your dosage allows. Your mission as a participant is to be open to either outcome and to dissociate from the stories of the mind. Ketamine allowed me to create a space between me, Irina, and all the triggers of the anxiety that I still had to process. It gave me the ability to understand that everything in my awareness is simply an unprocessed experience, now ready to be released and/or integrated into my current perception of self with acceptance and compassion.

The session lasted only 60 minutes. I felt fresh and renewed afterwards, writing the self-observations and insights that I witnessed in my short yet deep experience in my journal. Ketamine's gentle way showed me that it was time to let go of the energies, people and projects that I'd been invested in with the wrong intentions. When we operate from fear, we cling to life destructively. To be my healthy and authentic self, I had to choose myself above the world that I'd created and above the insecurities that helped me create that world.

Ketamine was the last slight turn of the key in my lock towards a happy and fulfilled life. Yet, was it the ketamine? Or was it my learnings from the intense initial experience with ayahuasca, combined with a stable and refined nervous system, a mind full of wisdom, and alert self-awareness that navigated me through the psychedelic journey itself?

I had to die again. Yet this time it was the most conscious death I've ever imagined. A conscious choice to be authentic, free, and powerful in my own nature. I've learned to adapt to daily life, accepting myself, allowing old parts of me to dissolve, and choosing to dance with the unknowns of life at every moment. Maybe you're there right now – fearful, doubtful of your own choices, feeling alone. I am speaking from a compassionate heart to those who feel incapable of choosing courage to move forward. I want to plant a seed of active hope that change is possible – not easy, but possible – and knowing that we own the power within.

About The Author

As an Awareness and Integration Coach, Irina's path is rooted in the discovery and exploration of the authentic self. After obtaining her coaching certification from the University of Miami and establishing her coaching practice, Irina travelled to the Himalayas, India, to study with living Masters and embody the ancient knowledge of Kriya yoga, pranayama and meditation. Her coaching style expanded into mindful practices, inviting her clients to combine the tools of Western psychology and Eastern philosophy.

Irina's personal story blends international roots, world travel, adversity, addiction and new beginnings. She desires to help those who have been suffering from disconnection and isolation, and ultimately contribute to building a healthier society. She continues her education in East-West Psychology at the California Institute of Integral Studies.

She leads psychedelic integration circles and psychedelic panel discussions to raise awareness around the power of the intentional use of psychedelic medicine to improve collective mental health conditions.

Connect with Irina Online: breathwise.co
On Instagram @coach.irinavlada
www.instagram.com/coach.irinavlada

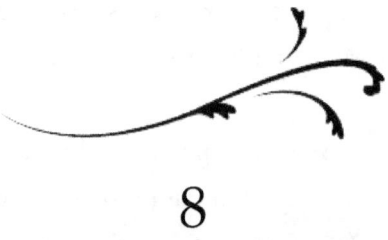

8

Ordeal, Death & Rebirth

The ordeal, death, and rebirth phase of the Hero's Journey is a moment of intense transformation where the hero must go through a symbolic death and rebirth to emerge as a new, transformed being. It involves the hero facing their greatest challenge and being tested to their limits.

Similarly, taking psychedelics or entering shamanic ceremonies can be seen as a symbolic death and rebirth experience as they confront and let go of old patterns of thought and behavior. In altered states of consciousness, individuals may experience a sense of ego dissolution, where their sense of self is temporarily dissolved or fragmented. This can be a challenging and disorienting experience, as individuals may feel like they are undergoing a true death and rebirth.

These altered states of consciousness can cause individuals to confront and shed their old identities, perceptions, and beliefs, paving the way for a new sense of self and perspective. This process of death and rebirth can be both disorienting and transformative.

As with the Hero's Journey, the experience of the ordeal, death, and rebirth phase can be transformative, leading to a greater sense of self-awareness and understanding of the interconnectedness of all things. Individuals may emerge from these experiences feeling renewed and transformed, with a greater sense of purpose and direction in life.

However, it's important to approach these experiences with caution and respect, as they can be intense and potentially challenging. It's crucial to seek out experienced practitioners who can offer guidance and support on the journey, and to ensure that the experience takes place in a safe and supportive environment.

Overall, the experience of the ordeal, death, and rebirth phase of the Hero's Journey and the experience of taking psychedelics or entering shamanic ceremonies share many similarities. Both involve a journey towards transformation and renewal, and both can be profound and life-changing experiences.

In our first story by American author Cindy Coats, after drinking ayahuasca, we see Cindy entering into the painful ordeals of revisiting traumatic memories from her past, an abortion she had in her twenties, and being in her mother's womb. She also learned that she herself had not been a mistake her young parents hadn't wanted and found new love and gratitude for them.

In the second story in this chapter, my own experience of ego death is shared.

Ego death

Ego dissolution, also known as ego death, is a common phenomenon that can occur during a psychedelic experience. It refers to a temporary loss of the sense of self or identity that one normally experiences, and can be accompanied by feelings of unity, interconnectedness, and transcendence, which can lead to a profound and transformative experience.

During an ego dissolution experience, a person may feel as though they are merging with their surroundings, losing a sense of boundaries between themselves and the world around them. They may also feel a sense of timelessness where past, present, and future all seem to blend together. Ego dissolution may also include a feeling of oneness with the universe, as well as a profound connection to other people and living beings.

This experience can be both exhilarating, awe-inspiring and terrifying, as it can challenge one's fundamental understanding of who they are and how they fit into the world. Some people may experience a sense of ego death or rebirth during this process, feeling as though they are shedding old patterns of thought and behavior and emerging with a new sense of self.

While ego dissolution can be a powerful and transformative experience, it can also be disorienting and overwhelming for some people. However, many people report that it ultimately leads to a sense of peace and acceptance, as they realize that their sense of self is merely a construct and that they are a part of something much larger than themselves. This can lead to a greater sense of interconnectedness and a desire to contribute to the greater good.

It is important to note that while ego dissolution can be a powerful and transformative experience, it is not always a comfortable one, and it can also be accompanied by feelings of anxiety or even panic. It is important to approach psychedelic experiences with caution and respect, and to ensure that one is in a safe and supportive environment with people they trust. It is also important to integrate any insights or experiences gained from psychedelics into one's daily life in a thoughtful and responsible manner. Therefore, it is important to approach the use of psychedelics with caution and in a safe and supportive environment.

Night of the Divine Feminine
By Cindy Coats

The third night of the ayahuasca ceremony at a retreat center in Costa Rica, involves "the night of the divine feminine." The ceremony is led by two female shamans, and it's designed to help men and women bring harmony to the feminine and masculine energy we all have inside.

I've always known I have a strong masculine side, so while I didn't know what was to come, I knew it would be a powerful night. It was the night I was most looking forward to.

Sometimes it takes an hour to feel the effects of drinking ayahuasca. This night, however, it took only a few minutes after drinking my shot glass of the bitter brew before I felt something stirring deep inside of me. I became filled with apprehension. Mother Ayahuasca always gives us what we need, which is not always what we want.

I wasn't sure where my visions were going to take me, but I wasn't ready. I was afraid of what the medicine was going to show me about myself. So, I sat upright with my eyes open for as long as I could. When I was too tired to sit up, I lay down with my eyes open. I had no concept of time. The room was dark, I had no watch, and the music hadn't yet begun. It became increasingly harder to keep my eyes open. Each time my eyes felt heavy and I momentarily allowed them to flutter shut, I felt a tightening in my chest, and fear gripped me.

When I could no longer keep my eyes open, I distracted myself with a trip to the bathroom. When they say, "Don't fight the medicine," it's not just because it's there for your highest and best good, it's because fighting it is futile! What Mother Ayahuasca wants to show you, she will show you.

I was sitting on the toilet when the visions began. I smelled antiseptic and when I closed my eyes, I saw brief flashes of a cold, sterile, operating room. When I stood up, I felt horrible cramps, as if my uterus and abdominal organs were being pulled out from between my legs. The vision had transported me to 1995 when I'd been almost 25 and woke up in the middle of an abortion.

It had been the most physically painful trauma I'd ever experienced. All these years, I'd put it to the back of my brain and ignored it.

I knew that I needed to follow the vision. After splashing water on my face and washing my hands several times, undoubtedly as a delay tactic, I finally returned to my mattress, lay down, and closed my eyes. The emotions I felt were overwhelming and unexpected. It was as though I was feeling the collective fear and sadness of every fetus ever removed from a womb.

I even sensed that some were old enough to have lived, yet had been left to die, alone, outside the womb. A deep feeling of guilt and sorrow fell over me. I've always prided myself on feeling all the feelings. I wasn't aware of just how much emotion I'd repressed around this choice. With my eyes closed, I cried and finally felt all the emotions I never allowed myself to feel back then.

At some point, I realized that I was no longer feeling my own emotions. The vision shifted and I was my younger self, a fetus in my mother's womb. The emotions I was feeling were my mother's. I felt the fear and uncertainty she'd felt, not knowing whether my dad was going to marry her or not. I felt her shame in having to tell her parents. I felt her morning sickness. And I felt the anger she'd had towards herself for having made such a mistake. I was the cause of her worry and pain. It was then that I realized I've always believed that I was her mistake.

A few months before my visit to Costa Rica, during ketamine-assisted therapy, I'd blurted out, "I am a mistake!" At the time I hadn't understood it. I'd always known that my parents hadn't planned me, but they'd never been anything but loving and kind and would have been horrified if they'd ever thought they'd given me the impression that I'd been a mistake or that they hadn't chosen me.

Even before we have words, even before we are born, we form beliefs. Because we don't have a fully developed brain, we don't yet have the cognitive ability to decide what is and is not true for us. For this reason, most of us are unconsciously carrying old, outdated beliefs — essentially lies.

Mother Ayahuasca was putting the pieces together and showing me the deep, unconscious, beliefs that I'd been carrying around my entire life. It's as though I'd known, as a fetus, that when I was born and out in the world I was going to have to hustle. I would have to prove to the world, my parents, and perhaps myself, that I was not a mistake. I would need to prove I was worthy of being chosen, worthy of love and belonging. I knew I was physically ready and strong enough to be born but I felt myself resist it to avoid the "hustle" that would be waiting for me.

Suddenly my vision changed back to the scene of my abortion and the physical and emotional pain that I was processing for the first time. I'd always said that if I could go back, I would make the same decision. However, feeling all the emotions I'd kept under lock and key for the first time, I had to wonder. It had certainly made the most sense at the time. I'd been young, and although my boyfriend at the time had offered to marry me and "give me a house

153

with a white picket fence," I couldn't see myself married to him. He was a British casino manager on the cruise ship I was working on. He'd always talked about getting a green card so he could work in the U.S. He would have done anything to get a green card... even marry me. It had never occurred to me even once that he might have been choosing me, choosing us. Although it didn't feel like a choice at the time, I ultimately did make a choice... I chose not to have a child.

With that, I was back in my mother's womb but this time I didn't feel any anger or shame, only love and gratitude for my parents. I also had such compassion for them at how young and scared they must have been. I thought about my dad who had just turned 24 and my mom who had just turned 25... almost the same age as I'd been when I was pregnant. My mother had had the same options as me – she could have given me up for adoption, she could have had an abortion, or she could choose to bring me into this world.

The power and repercussions of choice were suddenly clear, and I knew why I was reliving my abortion. I needed to see what not choosing a child really looked like.

Why hadn't I put those pieces together sooner? Because they were pieces of a puzzle I hadn't known existed; it was a belief I had no conscious awareness of. Anyone could see that my parents treasure having me as their daughter. The only one who couldn't see that was me as a tiny fetus. What does a fetus know anyway?

I didn't have to know anything, I only had to believe it enough for my ego to form... I became my ego, this other version of me who would do absolutely anything and everything, to feel worthy, to be chosen... even if it meant not choosing myself.

I thought about past relationships and the times I hadn't felt loved; the heartbreak I'd felt when I'd been left or cheated on... all the times I didn't feel like they were choosing me. Suddenly, it made sense. Buried deep below any conscious thought, my ego was holding onto the belief, "How could anyone choose a 'mistake', choose someone who hadn't even been chosen by her parents?"

This was a completely unconscious belief I'd been carrying around for 51 years without realizing the power it had in my life. Suddenly I could see that this unconscious belief was behind the pattern of my continually accepting less than I deserved in my romantic relationships. I could see where all my perfectionism and people-pleasing tendencies came from. I could see just how strong and powerful this belief had been, but I could also see now that this belief was all a LIE. I'd been WRONG all along. I had been chosen by my parents, I had been chosen to be part of this family. My parents have since told me that they never once considered any other choices. I HAD BEEN CHOSEN.

I felt the most immense love and gratitude toward my parents. As I bathed in the love and gratitude of this new awareness and belief, I had the compassion for myself to look deeper. I began to consider the soul/the child I hadn't chosen, whom I hadn't even had the courage to consider. I felt some of the most profound sadness I have ever felt.

I wonder how I could have felt absolutely no emotion at the time. I never shed a single tear back then. Now, 27 years of un-cried tears flowed out for what seemed like hours. I mourned the loss of the soul I would never know, I cried at the realization that the soul I didn't choose had been my only chance at motherhood. I cried for all the times I'd wanted to be a mother but believed I wasn't worthy because of my choice to have an abortion.

As I let new reality sink in, I suddenly felt like I was suffocating. I found myself gasping for breath and I felt like the walls were closing in on me. I fought to move my body and shake off this feeling, but was unable to. My entire body felt like it was being compressed. I realized I was in the birth canal. Without fear, I relaxed and was re-born. This time, I wasn't born with the belief that I was a mistake and wasn't chosen. This time, there was no knowledge of the hustle that would await me to prove I wasn't a mistake and prove I was worthy of being chosen. Instead, I was re-born with a whole new belief system. I was re-born knowing the TRUTH... I was chosen!

I was able to look back at past romantic relationships with new eyes. I could see that, at times, they really had loved me and had been choosing me, but my unconscious belief had prevented me from seeing it. Other times, I clearly hadn't been chosen by the men I'd loved and even been cheated on. Perhaps I'd been choosing men who weren't emotionally available, who weren't capable of choosing me or anyone else. I can never be certain of who did or did not choose me. However, I can see that I hadn't always been emotionally available because whether or not they'd chosen me, I hadn't chosen myself. My rebirth healed the core wound behind the bigger pattern of me not choosing myself.

There were times in my life when I didn't feel loved. As objectively as I thought I was looking, I only saw evidence that reinforced that belief. Through coaching and therapy, I learned, little by little, to shift my awareness and start looking for all the ways I was loved. To this day it's an intentional practice and does not come naturally.

I went to Costa Rica hoping to heal my heart where it had recently been broken. While I felt a little less tender and a little more

156

healed in that area, the medicine healed a much deeper part of me I hadn't known needed healing. I was able to see what true self-love looked like and what choosing myself looked like so I could see I hadn't been doing either.

Now, for the first time ever, I am choosing and loving myself. At times I wonder if I really uncovered and healed my core wound. I've often waited with bated breath for it to come back or wondered if there was another deeper wound lurking in the shadows. At this point, I don't know what else lies below the surface. So, I am continuing to journey inward to uncover more of what might be holding me back. But I will say this… in the months since this experience, so much has become clear. I am different. Something shifted and continues to be different – the way I speak to myself, what I see when I look in the mirror, the choices I make... I am not the same person after that ceremony that I was before.

I've since forgiven myself over and over for not knowing what I didn't know. I've also come a long way in forgiving others, who, like me, acted in ways they might not have otherwise if they had any awareness of their own core wounds. I can see now that they all, like me, had deeply buried unconscious beliefs. Some things still sting. Actions of people I care about will still impact me, but for the first time in my life, I can see that absolutely nothing is personal.

About The Author

Cindy Coats is a successful entrepreneur. She co-founded the real hot yoga franchise with the belief that, in addition to offering a means to stay fit, yoga communities can also be sanctuaries and places of healing.

When her boyfriend of 10 years had an affair and left her for a woman he met on a hiking trip, Cindy, devastated, found herself in need of her own healing and searching for answers and meaning in her life. In addition to the sanctuary of her yoga studio, she felt called to work with sacred plant medicine which revealed much deeper wounds than the one recently inflicted. A beautiful journey of healing, growth, and self-love began.

In her free time, Cindy enjoys yoga, cooking, traveling, biking in the mountains, and spending time with friends and family while also finding time each day for meditation, writing, and continuing her journey of growth.

Follow her on Instagram @rhyyogagirl

Purging My Old Identity and Being Reborn as 1Drea with Ayahuasca
By DaeEss 1Drea Pennington WASIO, MD

After sobbing in despair, asking God to take my life, I left my body and floated into a tunnel of light. Total peace, tranquility and calm was all that existed. I felt relief, as if God had finally agreed to free me from my physical existence. When I got to the other side of the tunnel I saw a full life review, and came to an understanding that all of the choices I made in my life since birth were the reason that I was so profoundly depressed.

That understanding seems so basic to me now. But at that moment I was shocked! I said to the peaceful spirit guide to my left, "I didn't know I could choose! Now that I do, I will choose differently." Another scene appeared in the dark void ahead, a scene of the Earth beautiful, blue, and seemingly ripe. Behind me and also to my left was a huge ball of golden light, like the sun, with tiny droplets of light emanating forth. As these droplets of light made their way to Earth I understood that they are us, little droplets of God, Source, Consciousness…

I saw that as these droplets of light consciousness reach the Earth we then incarnate into human form as little babies. It was clear to me that as drops of soul, we are the ones who are supposed to decide who we will be in life. It's not up to our parents, society, the media and certainly not the American medical system to decide what is right for our time on this planet. It was so beautiful and clear.

With the knowing that I can choose what I want to do in life I saw another scene unfold. As I shared in Chapter 1, the future scenario included me walking hand in hand with a child along the coast of the Mediterranean Sea. And in that vision, I was supremely happy and so was the child.

It was very interesting to me because up to that point I didn't even think I'd have children. I was single and 35, and I was ready to accept being childless. The vision seemed like a golden life and I said yes to it, which is when I was whisked back into my body lying on the bed in my hotel room in Cannes. Three months later I was pregnant.

For many reasons, the relationship with her father ended and I began preparing for life as a single mom. I said goodbye to working 80-hour weeks and closed my wellness center. I went to great lengths to being a super present mom, especially since I saw how my single mother's physical and emotional distance impacted me so profoundly. I studied attachment parenting as I didn't want to repeat the dynamic I grew up with. My little gift of life went with me everywhere and we were well-bonded. But I found it hard to cope with not working, not being super productive. I felt like my worth had evaporated and that I had become a milk factory.

My days consisted of waking up early to hydrate and nourish myself so that I produced enough milk for my sweet baby. Changing diapers, rocking her, and singing to her. Then feeding again. She was not great at sleeping in her bassinet, so I was soon exhausted with the routine. I found myself getting so frustrated and teary when I couldn't soothe her cries and couldn't get much sleep.

Her pediatrician said she was healthy, and that she would eventually sleep through the night, but after several months it just wasn't happening. Alone with the daily and nightly duties took a toll on my emotional health. I am ashamed to say there were nights I was filled with anger and resentment that my baby couldn't sleep without me by her side. After all of my life as a super achiever, I felt helpless and useless as a mom.

Uncovering my childhood wounds

I desperately called on my dear friend Celena for support. She too was a single mom of a young child and she seemed more grounded and tranquil than I was. She was living in Mexico teaching English and moved at a slower pace than when she and I worked together in my wellness center.

Celena invited me to leave the Washington DC madness and come to San Miguel de Allende, Mexico for a while. She convinced me that I could bask in the sun, enjoy a more relaxed lifestyle, write a new book and ease into motherhood with more support. So, with a toddler in tow, I traveled to Mexico where we lived for 6 months. I hired a nanny, who lovingly cooked for us and taught my daughter Spanish. I felt more relaxed and began hosting wellness retreats and teaching holistic health classes to the expats there while researching for a new book.

I met with a curandera who magically seemed to know me, though she had never seen me before. This wise healer seemed to hint at some hidden sickness in me, which scared me. I worried that I happened upon a fear monger, but in the coming months I felt a restless, unease bubbling under the surface. My daily routine of mothering and writing was interrupted by occasional bouts of frustration and anger.

My sweet little girl picked up on my edgy energy and became fussy. I quickly learned that I had to manage my mood or risk upsetting my daughter. Over the first three years of her life I saw a pattern, with the help of a wise therapist. Certain situations would trigger bouts of crying spells, irritation and self-criticism. With some introspection I understood that I was reacting with frustration at the very stages of development that I was either abandoned, wounded or neglected.

It became clear that my own inner toddler, a young, innocent version of me, was still inside me. As I gave my all to meet the needs of my outer child, my inner child was feeling something bad. Was it jealousy or resentment? Just the thought filled me with guilt and shame.

My research continued and led me to meditation practices for stressed caregivers, including the mettā or loving kindness meditation. The first time I practiced the mettā meditation, I felt relief as tears streamed down my face. Repeating the 4 simple phrases while directing loving, compassionate thoughts toward myself was foreign to my type A, perfectionistic self. But it was precisely the medicine I needed.

Following my destiny in France

Those 6 months in Mexico were a nice turning point for me as a mom. But Mexico was not my ultimate destination. Grateful for the respite Mexico gave me, and the new curiosity about indigenous healing, I returned to the US. Not long after, I attended the trance dance workshop I wrote about in Chapter 3 that further inspired me to clear out the emotional baggage of my past with the help of ayahuasca.

It took a few years to untangle my affairs and adjust to entrepreneurial life before I made the move to France. When I arrived at the Nice Airport in September of 2010, I had only my 4-year-old daughter and four huge suitcases with me. No friends or contacts on the French Riviera. And no job either. Just a vivid memory of a vision and a soul calling to live authentically.

My daily routine consisted of having breakfast with my daughter, taking her to school then practicing qigong and meditation — lots of mettā meditation. I was well-attuned to her needs, less reactive and a lot more playful.

Soon I began consulting with entrepreneurs who wanted to get more visibility for their personal brands and get published. I started a boutique consulting firm that over time grew into Make Your Mark Global, the publishing and personal branding company responsible for this book and 17 others. My branding consultancy brought me offers to speak on stages abroad, and I began offering retreats and workshops like I did in the US.

My daughter and I traveled together as I taught in England, Denmark, Iceland and India, giving us both rich opportunities to co-regulate our nervous systems and learn more yoga, mindfulness and meditation techniques. The happy vision I saw in 2005 had come true.

Internal turmoil returns

Around 2012, as my daughter entered her early teens, I saw more friction and tension show up in our daily interactions. I started to feel as if nothing I did was good enough. From the food I prepared to the music I played or songs I sang, there was an increasing expression of displeasure and boy, did I take it personally! I was struck by a mounting feeling of resentment.

My internal dialogue was one of a snotty list maker, counting all of the things I did for her, how hard I tried to make life special and abundant, and how much effort I made to do things better than my mom did for me. It took weeks of silent teary escapes to my bedroom, fuming with judgment at how ungrateful she was until I once again called on my soul sister, Celena.

I felt so ashamed for not being able to just give and do nice things without any expectation of thanks or recognition. After all, I thought that a good mom should provide and nurture without the need for praise.

Just being heard and understood and met with nonjudgmental acceptance allowed the inner shame and sadness to soften. I learned just how common it is for parents to feel that way. By getting past the 'shoulding' I was putting myself through, I entered into a state of acceptance and compassion for myself. Softening in that way opened my mind and heart.

A few years later I sat with psilocybin mushrooms I got another glimpse into my childhood that opened my eyes to the true source of my resentment. In a private healing session, I took a few grams of mushrooms accompanied by a playlist from my favorite medicine woman. The soothing mantras and melodic tones gently relaxed me as the mushrooms began to make the colors shimmer and brighten around me. Each time I closed my eyes and took a deep breath, I felt my body sink into the mattress — just like in my out of body experience. The boundaries of my physical self and my surroundings dissolved. Riding the waves of geometric patterns, swirls and twirls of moving colors, I relaxed into what would be a deeply cathartic journey.

I'm not sure how much time passed before the kaleidoscopic images turned into clear scenes from my teenage years. I saw myself around the age of 16 sitting on the bed in my bedroom. It was clear that I longed for attention, specifically the attention of my mother. At that time, she was running a very busy medical practice and rising up the ranks of the social scene in Denver, Colorado. I remember how sad I felt, because we didn't do anything together as a family. No meals, no movie nights, no hugs and no I love yous. Mom provided us with all the material things we needed, but next to nothing in terms of emotional connection.

Since my teens I always vowed that I'd never be like my mom if I ever had kids. And, indeed, when I became pregnant with my daughter, I began changing my life to fulfill that vow. So, moving to France and having made sacrifices to be fully present, the lack of appreciation I felt from my daughter stung. The mushrooms showed me that it was a part of me, my inner teenager, who was jealous of all the loving attention and care I lavished on my daughter. My inner teen was the part lashing out with anger and frustration when she perceived my daughter as being ungrateful.

Oh, how my inner teenager would have adored traveling the world, being closely bonded to my mother! In the scene I also saw how the loneliness drove me to look for love in all the wrong places. I could see why I ended up running with an unsafe crowd of girls from the other side of town. I understood why teenage me found herself living with her teenage friend, Charlene, and skipping school.

Under the effect of the mushrooms, I felt an intense wave of remorse and shame well up within me as I saw scenes from my time with Charlene. She was pregnant with her cocaine dealer's baby, and she was not able to quit the cocaine. I saw a mélange of scenes from that year where we got into many situations that were so dangerous. I folded myself into the fetal position and wept for the girl I was, the girl who was desperate for love, and who put herself in the most dire of situations.

I told my teenage self all the things I felt she needed to hear.

"I love you! It's awful that mom wasn't there for you. You do matter. You are worthy of love and attention. I forgive you. I'm so grateful that you are alive."

I saw my adult self snuggle up to my teenage self, and I gave her a huge hug. I told her that from now on she is not alone. I reassured her that she now has a dependable source of love and support. I could feel the hidden shame dissolve with my tears. As the journey ended, I reveled in how amazing it is that I didn't end up in jail, injured, abused or addicted as well. A major healing had taken place that was the first of many to come.

Reparenting myself

That mushroom journey, and dozens since, have given me an easy way to interact with the parts of myself that have held onto wounds from childhood along with limiting beliefs and unhealthy coping strategies. I find that sitting with psychedelics like psilocybin mushrooms, ketamine and ayahuasca open a window to the repressed content of the psyche, granting us access to the parts of ourselves that have been exiled to the shadows.

Richard Schwartz, the creator of Internal Fairy Systems explains that the use of psychedelics can help individuals access parts of themselves that may be difficult to reach in traditional therapy:

"Psychedelics can get to parts of the psyche that are usually too defended to access, and that can be very valuable. But if those parts aren't approached with an attitude of curiosity and compassion, they may just become more defended. That's where IFS comes in."

I have found that by combining IFS with psychedelic-assisted therapy and integration programs, we can gain a deeper understanding of the parts of themselves that may be holding us back or causing us pain. Through this understanding, we can work towards unburdening these exiled parts of ourselves and achieving a greater sense of wholeness and well-being.

As part of integrating this experience, I wrote in my journal every day and practiced the mettā meditation, showering my inner teenage self with loving kindness and compassion. I spent time connecting with that part of me and spoke to her throughout the day. I'd point out the beauty of the French Riviera and shared the pride and excitement I have for how our life has turned out.

Little by little, as I reparented my inner teenager I found my relationship with my daughter become smoother and sweeter. I felt far less of the need for praise or recognition for my motherly duties. I considered that everything I do for my daughter I'm also doing for my inner teenager. And I do it all with love.

IFS parts work combined with psychedelics can be a helpful approach to reparent ourselves. This lens helps us identify and heal parts of ourselves that may have been wounded or neglected in childhood. This can include parts that feel abandoned, unsupported, or unloved.

Through parts work, we can learn to access and understand these wounded parts of ourselves and provide the support and nurturing they need to heal. We can develop a compassionate and caring relationship with these parts, much like a loving parent would with a child.

Through the process of reparenting myself, I have further healed the wounds of my past and learned to live more fully in the present. I have developed a greater sense of self-compassion and self-love, and learned to be the nurturing and supportive parent to myself that I missed out on in childhood.

Purging guilt and shame and finding forgiveness with ayahuasca

After a year of deep healing with psilocybin ceremonies and parts work, I found myself thriving, enjoying a loving relationship with my daughter and inspired about life. But my newfound joy was not destined to last.

In 2021, during the COVID-19 pandemic I endured some major emotional shocks that inspired a new wave of deep healing. The first devastating blow to my mental wellbeing was learning that my mother had a stroke and was inches away from death. She had been rushed to the ER by my sister who told me she was unresponsive.

I spoke with the ICU doctor who told me it was pointless to get on a plane as I couldn't get into the hospital with the Covid restrictions. And worse yet, my mom would likely be dead by the time I arrived. I was knocked on my ass with waves of grief. While I had basically lost my mom a few years earlier as dementia took her mind, the news of her impending death made it more real.

A few weeks later I was hit with the news that my dear friend, colleague and soul sister, Celena, had died by suicide. She had suffered with some adverse reactions to benzodiazepines given to her for anxiety that tipped her into an emotional tailspin that she could not get out of. Despite residential treatment and many medications, she succumbed to a dreadful battle for peace. I was gutted. The friend who had so supported me and my transition into sacred healing work was gone.

I was fortunate to have 2 retreats booked in Costa Rica months later and the following year, which offered me the opportunity to sit with ayahuasca and yagé in 8 sacred ceremonies. I was ready for the deep dive and deep healing.

The first 4 ceremonies in 2021 were all about processing my grief of my mother's passing and healing more shame from my reckless teenage years. In one ceremony the medicine I once again saw scenes of my teenage years when I was not living with my mom. I was getting into trouble with the law and engaged in risky behavior. Even more deeply than when I took mushrooms with ayahuasca, this time I could feel the deep-seated shame and guilt I harbored for those days of frequent delinquency.

An amazing thing is that after the first cup my ayahuasca journey led me to call back my energy and soul fragments that were lost in my youth. I could see rays of light come back to my heart and my second chakra. Returned along with these pieces of my energy came glee, buoyancy and radiance to my heart and abdomen. I felt a sense of wholeness and rightness that was so new to me that I cried with tears of wonder and joy.

When I heard the call for the second cup, I couldn't imagine what more I would see or heal on the journey, but I gratefully received it. In my vision were the faces of my dearly departed friends, Meritxell, the Latin Queen of Soul with whom I sang in 2005 after my out-of-body experience. And then Dr. T, the supportive physician friend who always encouraged me to sing and not apologize for my abundance of talent. And finally, I saw sweet Celena.

Seeing her face in my vision brought a deep remorse to my heart. And while I found myself asking over and over why she left us, I also heard a judgmental tone to those questions. This led me to realize that I was holding a deep resentment towards her, and that recognition brought forth more feelings of shame. The anguish of knowing that deep within me I was secretly judging her moved me to ask for forgiveness, and helped me to forgive her.

As the medicine effects eased, I sat up on my mattress. Before the visions of each of these friends faded, I had made a vow to take action in my life to honor their memories. And as I hugged myself, I promised to follow through. And then a thought struck me. If I was visited by friends who had passed on, why had I not yet seen my mother? For weeks after her transition, I had dreams of her where she felt so close, so present.

With that thought I called out to her. "Mom, where are you?" Immediately a vision appeared before me. I saw a sweet little baby being born. I saw with 360 degrees of sight the parents and siblings of the precious newborn. And I knew then that my mother's soul was reincarnated.

Filled with tears of joy, I congratulated her. My mother loved life and given her traumatic childhood I was so happy to see that in the next life she would have a stable home and family life to set her up for a life of joy. This removed all sadness and grief about her passing. I truly feel she is in a better place.

I left that retreat with so much shame, guilt and judgment purged out of my sweat, tears and vomit, I thanked the Great Mother Ayahuasca once again.

My death and rebirth on ayahuasca

For the entire year after the retreat, I integrated the healing through journaling, connecting with my inner children, practicing breathwork and meditation, and enjoying a healthy relationship with my daughter. I also completed a fellowship in Psychedelic Assisted Therapy and received certification to facilitate sessions with ketamine, and psilocybin and MDMA when they become legal in the US.

The following year, 2022, I returned to Costa Rica as a guest speaker at an ayahuasca retreat center. And once again I drank the medicine. I didn't think I had much to heal that time since so much was released the year before. So, I went into the ceremonies with a general intention: show me what I need to see now. Simple.

Or so I thought.

One Ayahuasca ceremony took place on my birthday, November 9. After the first cup of the bitter brew, I didn't really feel anything, and I didn't have any visions. The second cup made me feel relaxed, but I felt as if there was something growing, an energy getting bigger within me. I explained to the shaman that I had no visions, had not yet purged, and wondered if maybe taking some hapé would help.

One of the people on the medicine team prepared the ashy tobacco snuff and blew it into my left nostril and then my right. An instant jolt of electricity shot through my nose and the back of my skull, electrifying my brain. I felt as though I was going to lift off the bench as I held on tight sitting before the medicine woman. She then began to recite a prayer, blew *Agua de Florida*, and passed feathers over my body, removing negative energies and illness.

171

In a moment I started to feel nauseous. It was a relief. Finally, I was going to purge. She handed me a bucket and once I purged, I regained my composure. I moved back to my mattress. But still, there's not much visual or mental material.

I asked for my third cup. Before she gave it to me, the ayahuasquera performed another blessing on me with chants, with *Agua de Florida*. I told her that the one thing that was happening at that moment was I was feeling a little guilty about my relationship with my daughter. There was something coming up around feeling really sorry that for those early years when I was so frustrated, and I felt like my behavior had somehow harmed her.

She asked how old my daughter is and I told her she's 16. She said, "Oh, you have so much time!" Then she gave me my next cup of Ayahuasca and said a prayer for me. I went back to my mattress after gulping down that acrid liquid. And sure enough, I started to see images of my daughter crying at various points in her life when she was sad, when she was mad, when she was frustrated. And some of those times I had lost my cool. I wasn't as loving and warm as I wanted to be. And I felt so guilty and ashamed and so remorseful.

Seeing those scenes made me cry and cry and cry. I felt so bad that maybe she was carrying sadness and wounds like those that I had healed from my own childhood with my strained relationship with my mother. I remember feeling like because I was replaying all of these negative scenes and feeling so bad, I was really afraid that in that medicine state, maybe my daughter back home in France could pick up on that energy. And so, I prayed to one of my Buddhist lineage protectors, the Green Tara. I prayed that she would put a veil of protection around my daughter so that she couldn't pick up on me working through the pain and the regret.

As the medicine really mounted in its intensity with the visions and just feeling so sick and full of regret, I heard a voice ask me, "Will you leave your daughter?" And in a vision, I saw myself far away on a path, wearing robes, almost like a Buddhist nun. I asked, "What do you mean, will I leave my daughter?" It reasoned, "Well, you feel like you've been a horrible mom, and maybe she's better off without you." But even that thought just made me cry out even more. And I heard it again, "Will you leave your daughter?"

I didn't understand it. So, I said no, and I just cried more. I apologized to my daughter. I hoped that I could send her my sincere apologies on a soul level in that medicine state. I never fully felt resolved that night.

On the following night, I was served yagé. Yagé is the Colombian brew, which is pretty much like Ayahuasca with some slight differences. When I went up for my second cup and once again explained that, "I'm not having any visions, I haven't purged, I feel stuck, and I'm really struggling with this inability to forgive myself with my daughter."

The medicine man that night remembered me from the previous year. Once again, I got a special healing with all of his magical tools and prayers. Then he gave me a cup. But this time it was different. It was much thicker. He said, "It's only a little bit. Drink it all and it's probably going to take you a while because it's thick." I held it up and waited and waited for the thick, sticky brew to get to the back of my throat. Grimacing and wincing with the horrible taste, I thanked him, and I thanked the medicine, and went back to my mattress.

Before I got to my mattress, the shaman told me, "When the medicine takes effect, when you're in that state, just send positive thoughts to your daughter." Within a few moments, the waves of nausea and sadness returned and once again, I saw visions of different scenes with me and my daughter. When it got really heavy, I did what he told me to do. I sent as many positive thoughts as I could, but I kept having this intense feeling of remorse as if I had broken her, as if the mistakes early in my parenting journey might have been imprinted on her in such a way that she's going to suffer in life.

Once again, when the medicine was at its peak, crying my eyes out, I heard again, "Will you leave your daughter?" I still didn't know what it meant, but once again, I saw this vision of me off in the distance, once again in robes. And I asked, "What's going to happen? Are you saying I'm going to go off and become a monk? Am I going to go crazy and have amnesia? What do you mean, leave my daughter?"

By this point, the anguish I was feeling was so intense and I could see no way out. So, I finally said yes. As soon as I agreed to leave my daughter inside my head, I felt the urge to vomit. I grabbed the bucket at the head of my mattress, and I puked. But it came from the depths of my soul, from the soles of my feet to the pit of my stomach and out and out and out. And it was as if this electricity was shooting through me.

As I was purging into the bucket, I knew I was purging a whole lifetime of experiences and *myself?* The third time that I was heaving what little was left in my stomach, I knew that I was not just purging my guilt, my remorse, but I was purging an entire identity. Somehow, I knew that after that experience, I wouldn't be the same person. I wouldn't be the same mother.

I moved away from the bucket and laid my head on the pillow. I was exhausted. Soon I saw this vision of myself. I saw myself as a little baby. There's this very familiar photo of me sitting on my dad's lap on a red velvet couch, I've got slobber coming out of one side of my mouth. And as a tiny baby, I just looked so innocent. And as I connected with that vision of little me, I said, "Oh, of course, I get it. I could see how you, as this tiny baby, you didn't stand a chance. You who absorbed the toxic fumes of negativity in our home. You who absorbed the electric zaps of confusion and drama and then moving away from your father and living in an emotionally distant relationship with your mother. Of course, you grew up to be the mom that I was!"

Suddenly, I could forgive. I could forgive that baby for she didn't choose to be mean or resentful. So many things happened to her that were beyond her control, so of course, I could forgive her! And so I wept and I cried and sent love to this little image of me. I told her I forgave her. I told her I love her, I told her I'm sorry. Pouring out all that love and compassion to baby me, I was finally able to feel lighter. It was as if I was finally setting free that little Andrea Pennington with all of her intergenerational trauma and karmic wounds. The heavy burden of her trauma left.

Visions of a bright future

Then I rolled over to the other side of the mattress and started seeing scenes of me and my daughter in the future, sitting at the dinner table, laughing, talking. My daughter is a total foodie. I saw that I could pour love into our meals and just be present with her and reconnect. And that vision gave me hope. I believed that I could repair our relationship and reparent her.

The words of the shaman were in my ears, "It's not too late. You have plenty of time". I knew that I was leaving a changed woman, a reborn woman. And I knew that I could never go by Andrea again. She's been set free.

On my way home to France, reflecting on all that had happened and feeling completely reborn, renewed, revitalized, I started to wonder, what name will I use? Ten years ago, I was given a Tibetan name by my Lama. I wondered, would that be my new name? But then I remembered after my singing in Saint Tropez in 2005, when I returned home after my mystical experience, I started to sing just like the vision showed me. And working with some hip producers from LA, I started playing with different names. That's where DaeEss 1Drea came in. After that out of body vision in France I knew that from that day forward, I would no longer be fragmented acting like a doctor on one day, a TV personality on another, a spiritual woo-woo person the next. There is and will always be only 1 Dreah.

And so on November 11, 2022 I was reborn and renamed DaeEss 1Drea.

I'm grateful that when I got home, my daughter told me she missed me. I grabbed her fast and held her in my arms. I am so grateful to have the opportunity to love her. And for as many years as she's under my roof, I will feed her. I will watch movies with her. We will play games. And I'll reparent her.

A few weeks after I got back. She did tell me that she could notice a difference in my behavior. And she wondered what was behind it. I explained a little bit. And she thanked me. And as she often does, she told me not to beat myself up, that I was a good mom. I am a good mom. I simply told her I can be better, and I'm going to be better. I want to be better because you deserve better. Now, here we are, six months after that experience, and we're as close as we've ever been. Happy. I even overheard her telling her friends that I'm cool. It was a painful idea to think of leaving my daughter, but that's ultimately what I had to do. I'm so grateful to be where I am today.

Internal Family Systems and Psychedelic Assisted Therapy

Internal Family Systems (IFS) therapy is a psychotherapeutic approach that views the mind as consisting of multiple parts or subpersonalities, each with its own unique set of beliefs, emotions, and behaviors. These parts are organized into a system that can be explored and understood to help individuals heal from past traumas, emotional wounds, and relationship issues.

IFS therapy involves working with the parts of the self that may be in conflict, and promoting communication and understanding between these parts. The therapist helps the client to identify and differentiate between the different parts, understand their roles and purposes, and work towards integrating them in a way that promotes wholeness and well-being.

The therapy typically involves three types of parts:

1. **Managers:** These parts are responsible for coping with external stressors and maintaining a sense of control over one's life.

2. **Exiles:** These parts carry the pain, trauma, or shame that a person has experienced and are typically pushed away or hidden from consciousness.

3. **Firefighters:** These parts are responsible for soothing or distracting from the pain of the exiled parts through impulsive or addictive behaviors such as substance use or compulsive eating.

IFS therapy can be used to treat a range of mental health issues, including anxiety, depression, trauma, eating disorders, and relationship problems. The approach emphasizes a compassionate and non-judgmental stance towards all parts of the self, even those that may be seen as negative or problematic.

Overall, IFS therapy is a promising approach for helping individuals achieve greater self-awareness, understanding, and wholeness, and for promoting healing from past emotional wounds and traumas.

IFS is now being used in combination with psychedelic-assisted therapy to facilitate deeper healing experiences. Richard Schwartz, the founder of IFS, now speaks about the effectiveness of using IFS in psychedelic-assisted therapy. He says that:

"Psychedelics can create an opening to the Self, and IFS can help people stay there, connect to it, and work with whatever comes up from there. Combining the two seems to be an optimal way of doing this work."

9

Reward

In the Hero's Journey, the Reward phase is a moment of triumph where the hero emerges victorious after completing their journey. The hero receives a reward, which can be material, emotional, or spiritual, and reflects the transformation they have undergone during their journey. This can be a moment of great satisfaction and celebration, as the hero emerges from their transformative journey with newfound knowledge, power, or insight.

Similarly, taking psychedelics or entering shamanic rituals can lead to a sense of reward or fulfillment. The altered states of consciousness that are accessed through these practices can provide individuals with a sense of spiritual, emotional, or psychological satisfaction. It can offer insights into oneself and the world, leading to a renewed sense of purpose and a deeper connection with the world around us.

The rewards of taking psychedelics or entering shamanic rituals can vary widely depending on the individual's set and setting, their intention, and the experiences they have during the journey. Some people may experience a sense of peace, connection, and oneness with the universe, while others may receive profound insights into their lives and the world around them. It could be connection with the Authentic Self, sovereignty, a secret, knowledge...

It's important to note that the reward phase of the Hero's Journey or the rewards of taking psychedelics or entering shamanic rituals are not the end of the journey. Rather, they mark the beginning of a new phase of life, where the hero or the individual must integrate the insights gained during their journey into their daily lives. This integration process can be challenging, but it is crucial for ensuring that the transformation experienced during the journey is lasting and meaningful.

Ultimately, the experience of reward in the Hero's Journey and altered states of consciousness can be a powerful motivator for personal growth and transformation, leading to a sense of empowerment and a renewed sense of purpose.

In our next story by Israeli author Chen Lizra, we see how the deep work of psychedelic journeys can lead to profound internal shifts and rewriting old narratives. Chen was introduced to ayahuasca at a retreat centre. She'd felt abandoned as a child by her mentally ill mother. Plant medicine gave her the perspective she needed as well as taught her how to find forgiveness for those who had hurt her. Chen explains how she uses somatic intelligence as part of her psychedelic integration work.

The last story in this chapter by John Jacob Mubarak demonstrates how letting go of old, outworn beliefs and patterns of behaviors can lead to rewards beyond belief. JJ worked at a retreat center in Costa Rica. It was here that he learned the secrets of giving and receiving blessings, and how we can all realize our infinite potential and unity with God.

181

Mom Left Me to Save Me
By Chen Lizra

When I was first introduced to Ayahuasca, it was by coincidence. I went to teach as a somatic coach at a retreat centre that offered Aya ceremonies and was offered the opportunity to participate in the ceremonies. To be honest, I was scared to join. My mom was mentally ill, and although I am not, I didn't have enough knowledge to really know if this could be dangerous for me or not.

So, I tipped-toed around the first night and only took the homeopathic version of the brew while being attentive to what was going on around me. I lay for hours on the mattress and waited for something to happen. Others around me were crying, purging, laughing… I felt in them a sense of calm around the room. The space was emotionally held by the shamans and helpers in a beautiful way. I felt safe. I felt the presence of deep wisdom.

Change starts with bravery

After a few hours, I mustered the courage and went to speak to one of the shamans. I told her that nothing was happening. She asked me if I wanted to try the plant medicine. I looked at her and asked, 'Do I?'

She said firmly, 'Yes you do!' I decided to try it.

I drank half the portion of the medicine then lay on my bed and waited. It took a while for it to kick in. Then I noticed that when my eyes were shut, I was seeing gorgeous visuals. When my eyes were open, I was in the room with everyone present. I closed and opened my eyes a few times switching between the two worlds.

It was intriguing. I then decided to go inward on this journey to see where it would take me.

I felt the feminine divine energy in my body – warm, fuzzy, loving and supported... it made me cry. I felt everything that I have ever missed from not having my mom by my side; the love, support, and comfort. The more I felt it, the more I cried. I cried for hours and hours on end, purging it all, while receiving the feeling of what my body truly craved.

Scared little girl

Then I saw myself at eleven years old. I was in bed and crying hysterically. I remembered this moment clearly. My mom lost control due to her mental illness and seconds before had hurt my brother, not understanding what she was doing. It became so scary that when she snapped out of it and I saw that he was okay, I ran to my room, fell on my bed, and cried for hours. My dog was beside me licking my face, and trying to comfort me and calm me down. I was hysterically terrified.

My mom came into my room. She was back to herself but she could not touch me. I would not let her after what had just happened. My trust in her was broken. Our mother-daughter bond was broken. She was helpless and didn't know what to do. I could feel her regret and shame so strongly.

Up to this point I remembered every detail that had taken place. That was when the plant medicine kicked in and caused a deep shift in my life. Mother Aya placed me both from the side as an adult, watching the scene, while simultaneously putting me in it as the eleven-year-old. I could feel all that I had felt in that moment in my body.

My body was shaking uncontrollably and all I wanted was my mom back the way she used to be. I was crying and shaking. I was terrified. I raised my head towards her and gave her a pleading look of "Mom, please come back, I need you." I begged her with my eyes to come back.

As a child, I'd felt like she had abandoned me. Yet this time, I didn't just feel it, I also saw it from the perspective of an adult, at the same time! What I saw was the look she gave me of 'I can't!' with a look of deep sorrow.

At that moment I realized something very important. She didn't abandon me. She showed the highest love as a mother – she sacrificed herself to protect us. She agreed to be taken to a mental hospital to be treated with electric shock therapy to protect her children because she realized she became dangerous to us. She loved me more than life itself.

I kept crying for a good few more hours till the medicine's effect wore off. My life has never been the same since.

The next day when I saw many of the participants walking around, some were panicked. I pulled those who were feeling that way aside one by one and did a quick natural healing session to create resonance within their nervous systems to help them process and release. Within a few minutes, they calmed down and were emotionally able to move forward from being stuck towards feeling good again.

What I did with them is a process called Witnessing. I connected my nervous system to theirs and felt in my body what they were feeling. This did two things - first, calmed their nervous system by being felt - the felt experience. Second, it allowed emotions that were trapped from past trauma to rise to the surface and be met and released. I was guiding them on how to discharge these emotions from the body so they can heal.

Emotions trapped in the body by trauma are hidden from us. We cannot come back to them alone and meet them. That's why we have shut them down in the first place - to protect ourselves - our nervous system could not integrate them back at the time.

As I felt them. They moved from panic to calmness within a few minutes.

A sweet participant said to me "I feel like you are an angel walking among us. You pull someone aside crying and they come back glowing." I smiled softly with love and pride hearing this.

Prepare well before partaking

Here is what I wish to say to those considering joining ceremony – you have to be ready for plant medicine journeys. They are not a small feat. They require preparation before and integration after. One of the most important skills is learning how to be with and move through uncomfortable emotions. Many people today have lost this basic human ability.

I can't emphasize enough how important it is to do the preparation work before attending Aya ceremonies, and just as important is also the integration work afterward. Many of us do not understand the wisdom of the body, what I call Somatic Intelligence, in order to integrate the beautiful lessons we receive. We can easily turn to anxiety or freak out, or even try to push through our emotions leading to numbness, especially when difficult emotions come to the surface out of nowhere. We can get overwhelmed if we don't have the emotional capacity or tools to hold space for this type of healthy processing.

Think of a three-year-old girl who feels something that is too much for her. The mother puts her on her chest and rocks her. The girl then feels the mother feeling her distress, and little by little she calms down. A few minutes later the crying stops and turns into laughter. She goes back to playing and enjoying the moment. The difficult emotion was released in a natural way.

Now, imagine if the mother wasn't there and these emotions came up over and over. How would she escape them? What would she lock up in her body to protect herself? And how easy or difficult would it be for her to learn to release these emotions again?

When we experience trauma this natural processing mechanism can get stuck. When we feel these difficult emotions, we then feel the urge to run to the other side of the planet. We hear a voice in our heads that says, "But why feel them if it never ends?" That's because we have lost the ability to discharge naturally. This can be healed and restored.

It's hard to be in excruciating pain, deep grief, and intense shame. When our nervous system feels emotions that are too big for us to process and integrate alone, if we are lucky, it automatically shuts down. If not, we might end up in a mental hospital or addicted to drugs, for example. As we grow older our nervous system matures and with it the capacity to sit with these difficult emotions. Yet it's scary to do so. They have now become a huge mountain we need to climb.

Observe the emotions – don t run from them

One of the things I teach my coaching clients is to not run. It's hard to sit calmly and feel difficult emotions. We tag them as negative or positive and try to discard the negative ones. Yet emotions are not positive or negative. Grief is not negative. Joy is not positive. They are just emotions that need to move through us. And what we need is the opposite in order to release and heal – we need to fully feel them to process them. This can be scary alone.

As a somatic coach, I look to dive deep into our generational and somatic imprint and to understand how we can heal it naturally. My journey started three decades ago with trying to find a way to heal myself first but continued as I wanted to save people from spending the three decades it had taken me so that they could do it in three to six months.

For this reason, and also out of curiosity, I keep exploring and learning ancient and embodied wisdom – things that are not common to hear about. That's where I find the deepest and most magical growth. And Aya ceremonies with the shamans have been one of my most powerful journeys to finding the truth. Witnessing has been the fastest way I found for healing our somatic body from the trauma. The trauma is always held both in the cognitive, the mind, and in the soma, the body.

I came out of this experience not only able to reclaim a part of myself and to heal a part of my own trauma, but also with a greater understanding of how the process works and how I can bring the embodied wisdom I know to help those who also wish to create such a deep shift in their lives.

Finding the ability to forgive

I'd like to conclude with my latest Aya journeys. In 2022, I felt like I was being summoned. After three years of feeling the inner calling to attend, I knew it was time! I needed to drink more medicine. And I knew exactly with whom I wanted to do this – the maestras from Peru who came from the divine feminine lineage and a deep, long lineage of natural healers.

This time I arrived with a clear question: how do I forgive the unforgivable? How do I forgive those who had knowingly hurt me in an abusive way? The ones that I just could not feel any empathy for. How could I release my rage for what was done to me?

I drank the medicine for three nights straight and went on a deep journey on the quest for answers. The entire first night I had to sit through intense rage in my body which felt like a 15 on a scale of 1 to 10! I was ready to explode.

On night two, I gained gorgeous insights on how to forgive each person I asked for wisdom about. On night three I was curled on the floor feeling excruciating pain the whole ceremony, for hours and hours. It felt like I was having a heart attack. Yet, I was calm and knew I wasn't. I felt I was ok.

I didn't understand why mother Aya held me in this pain for so many hours. I just knew that many times mother Aya gives us not what we want, but what we need. I respected this.

Many times, the wisdom unfolds in our lives not in that exact moment but when it's time for us to understand. We just have to be patient and let the unfolding take place, to trust in the process.

A few weeks after my journeys I mustered the courage to face the hardest case of 'forgiving the unforgivable' in my life. Out of respect for their privacy and considering that we are still processing this, I will not expose who they are and what the background history is.

After 18 years of not seeing them, I knocked on their door as mother Aya showed me in a vision. I was shaking with fear. I was about to face those who have hurt me profoundly. It led to an immediate conflict with them, then to an attempt at having some kind of a conversation, and me leaving with the situation unresolved. It was extremely difficult to stand in the situation and feel it all. I left feeling unresolved but hopeful that a conversation might take place, perhaps.

The interesting thing is what happened next. As I drove away after confronting them, I started crying. My body was releasing emotions uncontrollably. I felt intense pain for hours, exactly the same pain I felt as I was curled on the floor for hours in my Aya ceremony. I finally understood what mother Aya taught me – how to pass through it and not run. I allowed this excruciating pain to move through me, process and release for a few days. It was difficult yet it allowed me to finally heal.

I wouldn't have known how to do this had mother Aya not taught me by keeping me in it for so many hours. I feel grateful now that my rage is gone, my pain is gone, and the relationship has been rebuilding. Most importantly I feel at peace and was able to forgive the unforgivable.

Our ability to process, feel, witness one another, heal, relate to one another profoundly, and sit with difficult emotions are skills and embodied wisdom which are getting lost in the world today. We need to learn or relearn how to come back to the body, our primary home. I invite you on this beautiful and deep unfolding journey back to yourself.

About The Author

Chen Lizra has been helping change makers, coaches and executives return to their bodies, into alignment, and find their true selves through the Power of Somatic Intelligence. Based on her 25 years of experience and drawing on her own recovery from deep trauma, Chen has developed new techniques that are literally transforming people's lives every day by focusing on somatics, embodiment, and transformational coaching, combined with ancient wisdoms, in order to heal and restore the nervous system to its natural state.

In 2022, she launched the SI Wisdom Academy, a safe learning community for embodied change-makers, with profound wisdom and powerful somatic practices for achieving a new level of presence, resilience, and embodied impact. She has a specialty in the divine feminine energy with a massively popular TED talk boasting 12 million views. Chen was featured in the NYTimes, UK's Cosmopolitan and Lewis Howes' School of Greatness, to name a few.

Connect with Chen online:
Website: www.powerofsomaticintelligence.com
Facebook community:
https://www.facebook.com/groups/SabrosuraWisdom
Instagram: https://www.instagram.com/clizra/
LinkedIn Profile: https://www.linkedin.com/in/chenlizra/
YouTube Channel: https://www.youtube.com/user/clizra

The Blessing
By John Jacob Mubarak

At the time this story occurred, I had been working at a healing retreat center in Guanacaste, Costa Rica for about six months. Before my arrival I had lived in Los Angeles. I moved there in 2008 and was the sales manager at a charter yacht company in Marina del Rey, California.

Finding my spiritual home

During my time at the yacht company, I was introduced to the Agape International Spiritual Center by a soon-to-be dear friend named Stacy. I met Stacy sitting on the stoop outside my apartment building. Stacy and I hit it off immediately. One day she said, "Hey, I'm going to this place called Agape. I think you'd really like it. Do you want to come?" I said yes and the minute I walked in the door something was activated within me. I found my spiritual teacher and spiritual home at Agape. I volunteered and worked extensively in the community and in the offices of Rev. Michael Bernard Beckwith, eventually becoming an Agape Licensed Spiritual Practitioner.

A practitioner is a spiritual psychologist. We use the traditional modalities of psychology with the underpinning of the spiritual principle that underlying everything is a Presence of Love and Intelligence that is constantly seeking its own fulfillment through each of us. Fundamentally, Life is for us because Life is for Life, and we are part of Life! So, we can earnestly say that Life is Good, independent of circumstances.

191

Dealing with addictions and their roots

Ten years after meeting Stacy on the stoop, she called me. She was working and living in Costa Rica! She invited me to come to help start a new project at the retreat center. I arrived in 2017. During my ten years of study and practice at Agape, I had healed from long-time compulsive behaviors that had included a lot of sex and a lot of drugs. After moving to LA and joining the Agape Beloved Community, I cleaned myself up from the addiction and compulsive behaviors. It's important to know that no matter what addictive behavior we are working through, getting cleaned up from the addiction is only part of the work. The messier part of recovery is addressing the root causes of the addictive behaviors.

Addictive behaviors are like the floodwaters covering up all the stuff we don't want to deal with. After the floodwaters of addiction recede, what's left is a lot of mud and muck, and rebuilding that needs to be done. I had undergone huge expansions of consciousness at Agape. Yet, there was still a part of me that was absorbed with trying to fill a hole in the center of my being with external stuff. The hole in me was longing to be filled with self-love and self-acceptance, but I was looking for others to fill it with their acknowledgement or belonging. I was always "giving to get" and was very self-absorbed because I was constantly scanning my surroundings like a radar seeking the cues of acceptance and belonging from outside of me. The thing is, I didn't realize that I was doing this.

Finally, after six months at the center, I decided to try the plant medicine that was available there. I hadn't wanted to before because I had worked so hard not to have to take anything outside of myself to feel good. Yet, I had seen so many miraculous results week in and week out, I thought, "Why not, maybe it'll help." I had no idea how profoundly healing and beautiful my experience would be.

Most plant medicine ceremonies are held in what's called a maloca. This is a large, covered deck, filled with mattresses, blankets, pillows, buckets, candles, sacred objects, musical instruments, musicians, ayahuasqueros — the keepers of the medicine. Some call them shamans, but I am not a big fan of the word "shaman" because it has no etymological connection to the South American medicine tradition or native people. It stems from a Czarist Russian administrator's description of the medicine healers from Siberia to describe their unorthodox behavior.

Taking the medicine

I went in for the first night of the ceremony dressed in white and a little bit scared. As I entered the maloca, I chose my mattress and sat down. We were asked to observe the "noble silence" in preparation for the ceremony. There was an opening talk led by the ceremonial leader and then the call to line up to receive the medicine. At the center there are three group intentions. The first intention is: "Show me who I have become." That was my intention that night. This intention is meant to focus us on seeing the things that we typically don't want to see, hear, think, feel, or know about ourselves. "Who I have become" is the complex of defense mechanisms and projected self that we develop to protect ourselves. The things we do to feel loved, to feel like we belong, to feel safe and to feel enough.

I drank the medicine holding my intention in my heart, returned to my mattress, and waited. The first thing that happens when you drink ayahuasca is you begin to feel something in your body. I began to feel a little nauseous and to sweat, shake, and yawn. Soon the music was playing, and the ceremony was really getting underway. People were beginning to purge into their buckets. I noticed that as people purged, the ayahuasqueros would move throughout the maloca, assisting people by either giving them a blessing or a sort of energetic clearing and rubbing them down with this special lotion called Chandor.

I want a blessing too!

I didn't know much about it at the time, but I knew I wanted one of those blessings! I wanted a blessing because to me it meant that I had healed something. I was still looking outside myself to feel enough or satisfied with my efforts. As I continued to feel the effects of the medicine, I begin to see what are called pinta, which are geometric shapes and colors, kaleidoscope designs and tribal patterns – basically really cool stuff! I could also see the ayahuasqueros moving among the participants, administering their blessings and healings. Every time a healer walked towards me, I thought they were coming to give me a blessing. But they'd just walk by and work on someone else. This happened all night.

Remember, all of this wanting and not getting was under the auspices of the intention: show me who I have become. I did not yet realize it, but the medicine was showing me exactly who I had become. The coping mechanisms of feeling like I was enough through securing acknowledgement and external validation were being clearly shown to me. Also, my old narrative of feeling separate from people and life, or not belonging, was being shown to me through my growing desire for the blessing. There was also resentment and self-judgment that came up when I didn't get the blessing.

At the next ceremony, I went in with the same intention to see who I had become and with the added expectation that tonight, for sure, I will get my blessing! I drank the medicine, sat on my mattress and watched. The same process happened again and again. Something would happen in the maloca and the ayahuasqueros would move out into the group to give a blessing. It was so funny because it always seemed like they were walking towards me, but they would just walk right by. This continued until the third night. At this point, I was becoming resentful. I thought that the medicine wasn't working, and I felt embarrassed for even wanting a blessing so badly in the first place. It played into my old story that life passes me by, FOMO, and generally feeling like a victim.

This is the beauty of the medicine! It's always reflecting and revealing back to us the areas within us that are seeking to be healed. The feelings that this experience of watching the healers pass me by and wanting a blessing, the feelings of resentment and embarrassment, the feeling of victimhood – the medicine was reflecting back to me the areas within me that needed to be brought to the light. The feeling of not being enough; this story of being excluded; the need for validation from outside to feel like I belonged. These were all being healed in these ceremonies.

Now I see! Your blessing is my blessing

I began to observe these feelings and in the observation of them, something in me shifted. A thought suddenly occurred – straight from the medicine – and it said: "Their blessing is your blessing."

With this realization, I begin to celebrate! Suddenly, I wasn't waiting for a blessing to come to me. I could see the oneness in the room, and I KNEW I was a part of it and IT was EVERYTHING that I AM. I suddenly knew that if someone was healing, I was healing. If someone was getting a blessing, I was getting a blessing. If someone was being loved and cared for, I was being loved and cared for. A deep realization of the oneness of all of life filled me with joy! I began dancing on my mattress, rejoicing every time one of the healers passed me by as they went to give someone else a blessing. I felt like Oprah at an ayahuasca ceremony: *"YOU get a blessing, and YOU get a blessing, and YOU get a blessing!"*

As I was kneeling on my mattress with my eyes closed, dancing and swaying to the music, I was just feeling the blessings all around me. I opened my eyes and standing in front of me was one of the healers. He looked at me and said: "Brother, would you like a blessing?"

"YES! YES, I WOULD LIKE A BLESSING!", I replied. I received the richest, most wonderful blessing and experienced a deep-seated sense of oneness. During the blessing, I realized that there's only One Good. If it's good for someone else, it's good for me. I learned that I can rejoice in other people's success. I can rejoice in other people's good fortune. I can rejoice in other people's happiness. Because there's only one happiness, only one good fortune, only one success. I really learned that if one succeeds, it means we all can succeed! A deep realization that life is not a zero-sum game where one person wins and therefore the other one loses.

This was one of my first experiences with ayahuasca and to this day, the lesson of oneness and universal Good is still unfolding. This lesson is still being learned. It's so easy to forget that there's only one good. It's so easy to feel slighted or offended. It's so easy

196

to feel we didn't get what we deserved or just to feel upset because someone else is getting the credit for the work that we've done. Or, when things aren't going our way to feel somehow that good things are happening for other people but not for you or me. The lesson of oneness continues to be learned.

Navigating life with an awareness of oneness

In another ceremony, I was given a vision of many waterfalls lined up in this sort of half-moon shape. These waterfalls all flowed into one large river and, in the vision, that river was flowing over me. I was told that those waterfalls or headwaters were all of the intentions that I had set in each ceremony and that they were continuing to work and wash over me. The intentions that we set in a ceremony are always working. This is why we say that ceremony is only 50% of the work. The real work starts when we begin to integrate the insights and downloads that we received in ceremony into our everyday lives.

How do we navigate the game of life when it is played as if it were a zero-sum game? How do we move through life from the realization of oneness in a world where there are real winners and real losers? For me, the art of navigating life with the awareness of oneness is the art of denying what the five senses are telling me. Because the five senses are telling me that we are separate. The five senses are telling me that there are winners and losers. The five senses may be telling me that something's wrong, that there's a problem, or that the situation is hopeless.

The art of denying what the five senses are telling us is not a denial of "the facts" or sticking our heads into the sand. Rather, it is a complete acceptance of the present moment just as it is, whatever the circumstances. Why? Because even as we live in a win/lose world, we KNOW that there is only One Good and that Good is seeking to emerge. My job is to be open to receiving it in an unexpected way. It probably won't come in the way that I expect it. So, if I am feeling apart or separate, I have to do some work to remain open. I can't remain open if I am mired down in the muck of the same old limited thinking that got me there in the first place.

Whatever we are experiencing in this moment is the effect of our previously held thoughts, beliefs, opinions, perspectives, and points of view. Therefore, the experiences, feelings and emotions of this moment are inevitable. It is only from a place of complete acceptance of the now moment and of ourselves, exactly where we are at, that we can begin to co-create our next experience with the creative medium. The next now moment will be the effect of our current thoughts and beliefs. This is where we get to become the alchemists of our lives and turn the heavy leaden feelings of separation into the golden light of Oneness.

Viewing the physical through spiritual eyes

There is a saying: "Be in the world but not of it". The phrase has also been used in various spiritual teachings to convey the idea of detachment from material things and identification with a higher, more spiritual reality. Therefore, I can be in the world of a zero-sum game and at the same time I can be of the spiritual plane where there is no competition. I can choose to live in a world where everyone's blessing is my blessing and where everyone's win is my win and vice versa. As I cultivate the energy and awareness of oneness, more oneness shows up in my life.

Reward

It's like we must consciously say, "I am not in the matrix! I live and move and have my being in a realm where there is only abundance and oneness." It is from this upper room view that I can say that all that is rightfully mine comes to me with ease and grace in a magical way. I don't have to struggle or strive. I don't ever have to feel like I'm losing out. I can't ever lose because there's only One Good and your good is my good and my good is your good!

About The Author

John Jacob Mubarak is an author, Founder of Sacred Truth Tours, Agape Licensed Spiritual Practitioner, Elemental Rhythm Breathwork Facilitator, and Teacher in Residence at Rythmia Life Advancement.

John is committed to bringing joy and facilitating healing through the Sacred Truth Principles of Acceptance, Joy & Oneness. John's retreats, breathwork, teaching and private sessions activate spiritual growth and development for individuals to realize their infinite potential and oneness with God.

John works internationally leading workshops and retreats focused on individual transformation that creates the conditions for a world that works for the best and highest Good to emerge. When he is not leading retreats or being of service, you will find him in the jungles or on the beaches of Costa Rica – biking, hiking, camping, and living that sincere Pura Vida life!

Connect with John Jacob here:
https://www.johnjacobmubarak.com
Instagram: @JohnJacobMubarak
Email: johnjacob@johnjacobmubarak.com

PART 4
THE HERO'S RETURN

10

The Road Back

The Road Back phase in the Hero's Journey is a stage where the hero must return to the ordinary world, armed with newfound knowledge, power, or insight gained from their transformative journey. It is a moment of reflection and integration, as the hero prepares to bring their hard won understanding and abilities back to their community. This can be a challenging stage, as the hero must navigate the tension between their old self and their new self, and integrate their newfound knowledge and experience into their everyday life.

Similarly, coming out of a psychedelic experience or shamanic ceremony can be a moment of reflection and integration. After undergoing a profound transformation, individuals may need time to process and integrate their experience, and to make sense of how they can bring their newfound insights and abilities back to their daily life. It can be a challenging process of integration and re-entry into everyday existence. The altered state of consciousness experienced can be radically different from everyday reality, and the return to ordinary consciousness can be disorienting and overwhelming.

During this phase, individuals may struggle and may feel a sense of disconnect or alienation from their previous life and may need to make significant changes to their environment or social circle to support their new sense of self. They may need to confront the tension between their old self and their new self and make difficult choices about how to move forward in their lives.

At the same time, the Road Back phase can also be a moment of celebration and recognition. After undergoing a challenging and transformative journey, individuals may feel a sense of accomplishment and pride, as they prepare to return to their community with a newfound sense of clarity and purpose.

Ultimately, the Road Back phase is an essential part of the transformative journey, as it allows the hero or individual to fully integrate the lessons learned during the transformative experience and apply them to their everyday life. It can be a challenging and disorienting process, but it is also an opportunity for growth and personal transformation.

The next story is by American author Jeannine Sanderson, and it shows us how we could integrate new learnings into life going forward. Jeannine was sexually abused by her father from a very young age (she was just a baby). Her mother was no protection as she herself suffered from mental illness and violent fits of rage. As a teenager, Jeannine was in and out of psychiatric institutions, resulting in further trauma. Later, psilocybin helped her to create a new, better narrative of compassion, forgiveness, and joy. Her story inspires us to see a hopeful future life after deep work with psychedelics.

My Guide, My Golden Teacher
By Jeannine Sanderson

Like so many, my childhood was riddled with torment, torture, and trauma.

I was born to a father who learned early in life that sexual acts were one way to say, "I love you", even to your children. The first time my tiny body was ravaged to the point of needing medical attention, I was just six months old.

There would be many more trips to the doctors and extended hospital stays to come. In time, my young mind would learn to connect illness to safety. When I was unwell, my mother would come close, and my father would stay away. For a time, there would be nothing to fear. I remember becoming excited when my condition required a stay in the hospital. I knew I would be able to sleep in peace, never left to wonder when the door was going to crack open, letting in the sliver of light that always alerted me to the horrible experience that was to come. In the hospital, I was never alone; the nurses were gentle, caring, and attentive. It felt like Christmas morning to me.

My mother s inner demons

My mother also endured many years of untold trauma, abuse, and abandonment in her childhood, leading to mental illness which at times spilled over into violent episodes. It was easy to trigger my mother's rage. Her untreated illness, resentment, and guilt kept those powerful and dark emotions forever brewing just below the surface. It was not unheard of for my mother to pull a knife on someone who triggered her rage. While she never actually stabbed

204

anyone, on one occasion, when I was 11 years old, I was certain I was about to witness my mother murder the woman she felt had wronged her. I ran from the house in terror, screaming and crying for someone to help. Unfortunately, the neighbors knew enough of what happened behind closed doors that nobody wanted to get involved.

When I was a child, my mother would share stories of how she always wanted to have 12 children. She wanted to give her babies the love and the life that she always longed for, but she could never manage to climb out of her own suffering or release the triggers that took over the best of her intentions. That being said, there were moments of deep love and tenderness where I was able to connect with who she really wanted to be; who she really was beneath the fear and pain that she couldn't break free from.

Abandoned by our parents

My father left our family home when I began to menstruate, I was just shy of 12 years old. He told me that he was leaving because he couldn't stand to be around me anymore. It was several years before I'd realize that he was afraid of getting me pregnant. My mother left shortly after my father, often returning for only a day or two per week. She would come home to drop off some groceries, do some laundry, gather supplies, and check in on my brother and me.

I longed for the times when she came home and always wished that she would stay just a little longer. I wanted to beg her to stay, I wanted to tell her how much I needed her, and I wanted to tell her that I was afraid, but I had made that mistake once before.

She came home without warning one evening. I had been sitting alone watching TV. It was after dark, and all my friends were at home with their families for the night. I jumped up excitedly when I heard the door open. I ran to give her a hug and let her know I was so happy to see her. She told me that she was just home long enough to change her clothes and she would be leaving again. I told her I was lonely and afraid and asked her what her friends had that I didn't, and why couldn't she stay with me. Her response ensured I would never ask her to be a mother to me again.

She told me that she couldn't stay and that by asking I was making her feel guilty. She changed her clothes, grabbed her keys, and headed towards the door, but stopped to tell me, "I'm going to hit the nearest bridge at 90". She got into the car as I watched in terror. What had I done? She left in a cloud of dust, throwing gravel with her tires as she sped away. I sat alone, sobbing until I finally fell asleep. It would be days before I saw her again to know that she was okay.

A crack in the facade

The sexual, physical, mental, and emotional wounds created by many years of abuse led to regular bouts of illness and injury. I was left with physical scars and internal damage that required multiple surgeries to correct. In my teens, I was told that my chances of ever having children were very slim. With this news, I went on a merciless rampage of self-abuse. Years of self-destructive behaviour that included self-mutilation, eating disorders, self-endangerment, and multiple suicide attempts. I was finally noticed and labeled a "youth at risk".

I spent a significant amount of time as a teenager going in and out of psychiatric units and hospitals. Looking back, the treatment for trauma at that time was traumatizing in and of itself. The psychiatric hospitals were often filled with youth who had been court-ordered into custody for criminal behaviour. During one stay, I was the only patient who wasn't there due to committing a crime. This meant that there was no treatment for trauma or abuse.

As punishment for non-compliance, I was locked in an empty room with a large metal door and a window that had a screen made of thick metal wire placed so closely together that you could barely catch a glimpse of the outside. This room was referred to as the Quiet Room, an intense time-out of sorts.

I don't remember all the incidents that landed me in that horrible room but there is one I will never forget. I refused to remove my oversized T-shirt that was covering my bathing suit. I wouldn't expose my nearly naked body in front of others. I was embarrassed, ashamed, and afraid that somehow everyone would know everything. On this occasion, I spent several hours locked in that room. I couldn't understand what I had done that was so wrong or why nobody was able to save me. I was convinced that I was worthless.

When I wasn't being assaulted at the hands of another, my mind would take over to horribly abuse me. My thoughts were as cruel and unrelenting as any external assault I had endured. Being present inside my head was difficult, but reaching out for help seemed a far worse fate. The abuse felt never-ending, and I longed to be set free. While I was physically, mentally, and emotionally unwell, my intelligence remained perfectly intact. I began to seek and study all I could find on psychology and mastering the mind. If I was to make it out alive, I knew I had to save myself.

A ray of light in the face of darkness

While in college, the almost impossible occurred: I became pregnant. It was a miracle, and I was so excited. That is, right up until the day my son was born. When I laid my eyes on that perfect little being, my heart broke and tears streamed down my face as I sobbed. I knew my family history, I knew where I had come from, I knew all I had to offer was all I had to give and that wasn't good. I loved him far too much to destroy him. I knew what I had to do, I had to give him up. I refused to hold him, I just couldn't. I turned away from my beautiful baby and wished that I could die, life was just too cruel.

Despite my refusal, the nurse placed my helpless baby on my chest and let him go. I instantly wrapped my arms around my tiny son, and that was all it took. I didn't know how I was going to do it, but I knew nobody could ever love him as I did. I had never felt an all-encompassing love like that, my heart was so full. To say that I would die for him was not untrue, but the greatest testament of love would be to live for him. I promised him then that I would never let go; I would instead work tirelessly to rise.

In time, my coping skills grew, and I was able to function well enough to live a relatively normal life. I continued exploring multiple treatment methods for c-PTSD in an attempt to find an effective way to calm the occasional raging storm inside my head.

I knew what it was to exist; I did that daily. But I was afraid much of the time. I wanted to know what it was to live, to have a safe space, even if that space only existed within my mind... Certainly, I deserved that and I felt it had to be possible. Even if it wasn't, I had to believe it was because seeking and finding, learning, and growing was something I could do well. This belief gave me unshakable hope and incredible drive.

Some methods were more effective than others. After much exploration, I found that my life worked best when I combined a regular routine of self-hypnosis, meditation, energy healing, proper diet, exercise, and detox. My life had changed so significantly that I thought I had achieved the best I could expect, and I began creating a life that allowed me to share all I had come to know along my journey, and that generated even greater healing.

My mother s caregiver

Many years later, I would be called to be my mother's keeper as dementia ravaged her body and mind. This created new trauma and unearthed some distant shadows that were still lurking. My mother and I had worked for many years to create a relationship that was mostly safe, and that I was willing to participate in. With relatively clear and manageable boundaries and deep understanding, it worked well enough. But that was before dementia took my mother back in time and brought some of the old mental, emotional, and physical abuse back to the surface.

Memories of some deeply buried events, which still haunted me, began to surface. Flashbacks so dark, shameful, and unforgiving that, when triggered, had the ability to knock me to my knees, rob me of my breath, flush my skin and cause my heart to race. I had always known there were still some secrets buried deep, but I could never quite reach them. My true liberation felt always just beyond my grasp... until my experience with psilocybin-assisted therapy.

Under the influence of sacred medicine

I was never opposed to psilocybin therapy; I had just never considered it for myself. I really didn't think I needed it. After all, I was doing great.

As my mother's live-in caregiver, I stood in the face of the barrage of verbal, mental, emotional, and even physical abuse for a time, until I would finally crumble and break down. More and more often I was having to remove myself, to barricade myself away as a form of protection. More and more I was locking myself in a room, curling into a ball and silently sobbing. More and more I was reliving my past and feeling trapped despite my best efforts. I remember praying to God for guidance. I had dedicated so much of the first part of my life to finding ways to climb out of my personal hell; I just couldn't let myself go back to where I had been. In the years since my last deep dive into treatments for c-PTSD, magic mushrooms had been making headlines, and I was ready to embrace the experience.

While under the influence of psilocybin, I could stay present and go into some deep memories, to gain greater insight and understanding of the impact they'd had and the triggers they'd left behind. It was like psilocybin was a key that opened a sealed door, allowing me to truly see for the first time ever.

I went through a cascade of memories, emotions, and the meaning they were given by one far too young to be able to grasp what was happening or how to cope. My heart hurt for that beautiful little girl and for all the broken adults around her who didn't give what she so richly deserved and needed. I understood that they didn't have it to give because there had been no one able to give it to them and I felt compassion.

As I spent time looking at my mother's deeply traumatic past, I began to almost automatically experience a level of self-forgiveness, self-love, and compassion that I lacked, and didn't know was possible.

As I forgave my mother for her mistakes, I was forgiving one of the major sources of my faulty programs. And, like all things, when you heal the source, the symptoms begin to ease. As I forgave my mother and the trauma programs that I had absorbed from her were set free, I became automatically more authentically me.

I felt grateful I was experiencing this now; that I was being provided with this opportunity for deep compassionate understanding, healing, and peace. I also recognized that I was experiencing deep healing that my parents had never been able to.

Changing my old narratives

One of the most amazing aspects of psilocybin-assisted therapy for me was that I could easily witness past events from an observational standpoint. I had such compassion, understanding, and grace... such pure love for every version of me and every emotion I experienced. For all I went through, for the parts of me that in turn hurt myself and others, for all that had been lost, all the opportunities I would never experience because of the torture that was endured and the reactivity that was left in its wake. I could stay present and send love to the anger, to the fear, to the shame, to the hope, to the perseverance, to the will and determination, to the seeker who got us from there to here, even through all her fear.

Many narratives were exposed and rapidly altered, instantly becoming lighter, more compassionate, and more truthful. Things I had previously had an intellectual grasp of, I now had a felt sense of.

I was later able to use that experiential knowledge to help me remain conscious and rise above remaining triggers in my everyday life. I was more easily able to observe from a place of awareness and empowerment rather than to be pulled into the past and the automatic responses that were created to survive. I cried, forgave, released, laughed, and felt deep inner peace, security, and connection. I felt my authentic self and she was beautiful; I was pure love and compassion. I can go back there in my mind and feel it all over again, and I do almost daily.

The steps beyond the psilocybin therapy sessions haven't all been completely comfortable but, with a new narrative, deep compassion, and awareness, even the challenging steps have been clearer and more manageable. When I catch myself stumbling, when the triggers attempt to take over the truth, it is almost automatic for me to pause, reflect, reframe, and choose peace. I AM absolutely in love with the continual growth and the joy that I find within it. It has made me a better partner, friend, mother, and therapist.

I have stated on multiple occasions that in my experience, one single session of psilocybin-assisted therapy was more effective than years of traditional therapy. Words are a thousand times too small to express how this therapy altered my life. As it brought me closer to myself, it brought me even closer to my creator. I have a deeper and more personal relationship with the source than I have ever had before, and my faith has always been strong.

When I was a teenager, each time I would pass by a cemetery I would think, and often say, "Look, my dream home". Now I know what it is to live authentically and even in challenging times, I look forward to living every day. I can't even imagine what incredible experiences and growth spurts lie just around the bend, but I look forward to being present with each one.

It is my sincere hope that this powerful sacred medicine becomes an option for all who wish to try it.

About The Author

Jeannine Sanderson is a hypnotherapist, hypnotherapy instructor, reiki master teacher, author, and speaker from Canada.

Jeannine is no stranger to adversity. Childhood traumas left her with depression, anxiety, and suicidal ideation. Early on, Jeannine discovered that traditional treatments for mental illness were not enough to create the inner peace she yearned for.

Along her personal quest for healing, Jeannine discovered hypnotherapy and subconscious reprogramming. Through these, she learned how to take control of the triggers and automatic responses that had held her prisoner to her past.

Through releasing her suffering, Jeannine discovered her true calling and genuine passion to aid people in overcoming life's challenges holistically. She incorporates multiple healing modalities to empower her clients to transform their lives.

Jeannine specializes in teaching subconscious reprogramming and personal empowerment through hypnotherapy and international well-being workshops. She also offers hypnotherapy certification courses.

Connect with Jeannine Sanderson at:
Web: www.essentialmindmatters.com
Facebook: www.facebook.com/EssentialMindHypnosis/

Psilocybin Mushroom Strains

While psilocybin mushrooms contain the same active ingredient, psilocybin, different strains of mushrooms can have varying effects due to differences in their genetic makeup and the specific concentrations of psilocybin and other psychoactive compounds.

Here are some examples of different strains of psilocybin mushrooms and their reported effects:

Golden Teacher: This strain is known for its spiritual and introspective effects, often inducing a feeling of connectedness to the universe and a sense of clarity and insight.

Penis Envy: This strain is known for its high potency, often resulting in a more intense and longer-lasting trip compared to other strains. It can also be associated with a more introspective and emotional experience.

White Albino: This strain is known for its visual effects, often inducing vivid colors, patterns, and distortions in perception. It is also reported to have a euphoric and energizing effect.

Liberty Caps: This strain is native to Europe and is known for its intense visual and auditory hallucinations, often described as a "surreal" or "dream-like" experience. It can also be associated with feelings of euphoria and a sense of spiritual connection.

B+: This strain is known for producing a warm and uplifting trip, often accompanied by feelings of euphoria and relaxation.

Ecuadorian: This strain is known for producing a more intense and long-lasting trip compared to other strains, often resulting in vivid visual and auditory hallucinations.

Mazatapec: This strain is known for its gentle and relaxing effects, often inducing a feeling of peace and tranquility.

Amazonian: This strain is known for its potent and euphoric effects, often associated with a more intense and emotional experience.

It's important to note that the effects of psilocybin mushrooms can vary depending on factors such as the user's mindset and environment, dosage, and other individual factors. Additionally, the use of psilocybin mushrooms can be risky and potentially dangerous, especially if used without proper preparation and guidance from an experienced practitioner. Some of the reported risks associated with the use of psilocybin mushrooms include psychological distress, paranoia, and the potential for accidents or risky behavior while under the influence of the drug.

11

Resurrection

The Resurrection stage in the Hero's Journey is a moment of rebirth, where the hero undergoes a final challenge or obstacle that tests their newfound abilities and strength. It is a moment of transformation, where the hero must confront their deepest fears and weaknesses in order to emerge stronger and more empowered.

Similarly, taking psychedelics or entering shamanic ceremonies can be a moment of rebirth or transformation. These experiences can bring individuals face to face with their deepest fears, insecurities, and obstacles, forcing them to confront and overcome these challenges in order to emerge stronger and more empowered.

In altered states of consciousness, individuals may experience a sense of ego dissolution, where their sense of self dissolves and they are confronted with the true nature of their being. This can be a challenging and transformative experience, as individuals must navigate their way through the unknown and face their deepest fears and vulnerabilities in order to emerge transformed.

The experience of resurrection in altered states of consciousness can be a moment of profound insight and clarity, as individuals confront and overcome long held wounds and vulnerabilities. They may feel a sense of rebirth or renewal, as they emerge from the experience with a renewed sense of purpose and clarity.

However, it's important to note that the experience of resurrection in altered states of consciousness is not always guaranteed. These experiences can be challenging and unpredictable, and individuals may need to work with experienced practitioners to ensure a safe and transformative experience.

Ultimately, the experience of resurrection in altered states of consciousness can be a powerful reminder of the transformative potential of these experiences, and of the inner strength and resilience that lies within all of us.

In our next story by Dutch author Myrthe de Jongh, we learn how seeing hidden memories from her childhood led to a rebirth of self-acceptance. Myrthe had issues with sex addiction which she used as a tool to be seen and loved. After discovering Mother Ayahuasca, she finally felt loved and fully accepted for who she was. As with many others who use plant medicine, memories of abuse surfaced. Today, from her hometown in the Netherlands, Myrthe helps others to choose love over fear.

In our last story in this chapter, American author Niki paints a different picture of resurrection. Although Niki had grown up with an awareness of Mother Nature and her gifts, that didn't stop her from having deep emotional issues. Most of these stemmed from her father's absence while she'd been growing up. Niki self-medicated with multiple drugs from the age of 15. Her addiction culminated with a suicide attempt. Then she found psilocybin and a new way of living.

How My Biggest Pain Became My Greatest Gift
By Myrthe de Jongh

Hello, beautiful soul. My name is Myrthe de Jongh and I'm living in the Netherlands. The day before writing this story I guided a private ceremony with ayahuasca. I woke up at 06.06 and somehow I looked at my phone and came across Andrea Pennington's profile. (She is now known as DaeEss 1Drea.)

Next came the call to share my story with plant medicine. For a while, I've been feeling this excitement and have been ready to get into the world with my stories and knowledge. Do you believe in coincidence? I don't. So here I am, sharing my story. I want to thank you for reading all these beautiful stories in the first place and wish you many blessings for your own unique journey!

Plant medicine changed my life and I'm feeling so blessed to be working with it to help change others' lives as well. However, it didn't and still doesn't happen without my own commitment to my healing process with the love for integrating life in all different aspects. All the dark and the light. All the lessons and all the celebrations. This is what I also bring into the consciousness of the people that I guide. Because we can have the deepest healing and wonderful experiences in our psychedelic journey. But then what? Life happens. And life happens hard and fast when you're not aware or not giving yourself the permission to have loving awareness towards it.

Mother calling to me

My own journey with ayahuasca started about five years ago. Maybe you have heard something like, 'You need to get the call'. The call? What is the call, right? I love to mention this one because sometimes I see people and they're feeling the urge to connect with ayahuasca but haven't received their 'call' yet. In my opinion, it's a call from within yourself, your intuition, that is simultaneously connected with all the energy inside you and around you. It's all connected like we are as well.

You may get similar experiences that keep reminding you of the medicine, more and more often. You hear people talking about it, read messages about it, etc. This is how it worked for me: A friend of mine shared about it, and then another person and another. It came into my field. Into my consciousness. Then, I started to get a feeling about it. A tingling, curious and thrilling feeling.

It is now January 2023. New year, new possibilities. New possibilities are what came with my healing journey and my connection with plant medicine. The woman I was about 10 years ago was a whole other person with a different perspective of myself, life and others. I was the queen of abandonment. Running away from my feelings; hiding and distancing myself from my body. I gave myself away and actually abused my own life energy.

All this came from deep-rooted trauma in my unconscious body. I had different kinds of therapy and was also in a clinic for love/sex addiction. I used sex/love as a tool to be seen and loved. Back then that was what I thought was the main reason for my complex behaviour. I tried and I tried. I cried and I cried. I always ended up hurt and feeling unworthy. The superficial connections and the ones where I was pleasing and trying to fix everything were

221

leaving me with even more emptiness and disappointment. I remember the words that a friend of mine once said to me, 'Myrthe, there are more things in life than men'. I felt those words. Because yes, that seemed like the only thing that mattered.

Honesty and authenticity

My big turning point came when I read about addictions in a magazine. I felt so much recognition. It was confronting but immediately I felt my call to action. That was a rough journey for me. I had to share this with people close to me, my friends and family. I also had to work because I needed extra days off to get into rehab. I felt a lot of shame but I never ran away from my authentic story. I feel grateful for the people close to me who supported me. Many people didn't understand or were shocked. But I knew I had to do this for ME. I felt a strong urge to keep on going, to understand and free myself. Maybe the rebel in me that I created in my teenage years was a pretty badass girl that kept me there.

These therapies gave me a lot but not the deep healing and opening that I needed to get to where I am today. I felt like there was something hidden deeply, and I couldn't get there. I felt stuck. My whole perspective changed about the addiction because I never knew what lay underneath it until I met Mother Ayahuasca.

My first ceremony

Despite many mixed feelings, with an excitement in my belly, I decided to book an ayahuasca ceremony. It felt scary because it was a big leap into the unknown. What if something comes up that I can't handle? Or what if I lose myself?' At the same time, it felt like the right thing to do.

I'd like to invite you in this moment while you are reading to feel with me. Because wow! While writing this, the tears are strolling down my face. This is a memorable moment for me. It's so deeply connected to feeling how much ayahuasca means to me. How stuck I probably still would have been with all my toxic relationships, low self-worth, scarcity, and small amount of self-love.

During all my ceremonies, despite how hard and painful they sometimes were because of all the pain that wanted to be seen, felt and released, I felt the warmth and love of Mother Ayahuasca and her spirit. It felt like a warm hug, and she always gave me the courage to move through it. This was something I needed the most because the safe feeling in myself was far away. Mostly there was a beautiful light in the tunnel and if there wasn't, it was okay because I felt a lot of trust. There were deep life lessons, spiritual awakenings and connecting with the most unconditional love I had ever felt.

I remember my first ceremony. I went with a friend of mine. We went to the house of two loving people who would be guiding us and the other four participants. I was so nervous but said, 'Okay, let's go'.

In my white clothes, I drank the brewed tea that tasted very earthy. I lay down on a mattress, the music started to play, and my journey began. What I remember the most was that I was fighting against myself. Letting go of control felt so unsafe. I remember that the ceremony guide laid his hand on my chest and said to me, 'You are the only one who can open the door'. This was exactly what I needed. It was as if he could directly feel what I needed at that moment. I felt so scared for what may come when I opened that door, but I took the little girl inside me by the hand, took a deep breath, and surrendered. And that was where it all started.

Memories of abuse surface

I've come so far. There are many different reasons but to stick with the topic, it's because the safety in my body wasn't there. After my first ceremony where I was mostly fighting with my inner self, I still had that feeling of something stuck in my stomach. Soon after that ceremony, I went for the second time. Ayahuasca showed me in small snapshots of visions that I'd been abused by my father. That was the most shocking thing I'd ever experienced because I hadn't been aware of it until that ceremony. However, at the same time, it made so many things so clear. It was as if the puzzle fell into place and until today in 2023, there are still pieces that are falling into place during my personal life journey.

The newfound safety in my body and the guidance into this for others is one of my biggest gifts now. Knowing that this is such a deep trauma that it still can come to the surface sometimes feels just like the urge to distance myself does. These are old mechanisms that can be triggered during some situations but mostly I am aware of them, and they don't control me anymore. This is where conscious integration is so important – knowing how to navigate through these feelings and holding myself in them. It took me a while and a lot of patience. Practicing patience, love and softness is what I experienced in many ceremonies but also what is the basis of life's practice.

From here I finally had the possibility to really work with this big theme of my life. That was a big part of the integration. I broke the connection with my dad. It was a hard thing to do but in the end, I realized that throughout my whole life, he'd never really been there. The memories of a weird feeling in my stomach when I was with him came to the surface as well.

When it felt right, I did another ceremony to heal this area even deeper. I chose a good therapist who guided me through this, and after this healing process she also taught me how to work with these topics in my own coaching business. It involved healing as well as opening up in sensuality and sexuality with a touch of Tantra and Taoism. Plus, I truly love to combine that with the shamanic essence of plant medicine. Yes, a big part of my life's purpose and mission was born. I've never felt so radiant and free!

Freedom through nature s gifts

This is what I want for everyone – to be free from trauma. Old patterns and blockages are what are keeping you small and away from who you truly are. Our essence is full of love, freedom and sexual energy. It's your creative life energy that is abundantly flowing and growing inside and around you once you notice and open up to it.

Plant medicines are such a gift from nature. They give us the opportunity to heal ourselves and create new frequencies and possibilities. We can open to the magic when we stop blocking all these untouchable things with our minds. These come from fear. And yes, I see you and I feel you when you are still experiencing a lot of fear. But you can give it a try.

During the years of doing my inner work supported by plant medicine and a lot of self-practice and guidance from coaches, I've become way more spiritually aware and open in energy healing work. This is an extra layer in the plant ceremonies that I guide. In my daily life and the ceremonies, I receive the medicine myself. It opens new possibilities in connecting with the energy inside and outside ourselves. The more we open ourselves, the more we become capable of healing ourselves because we become aware of our energy, our body and how everything is connected. We feel, then we let go or accept and move into new perspectives.

I still feel surprised by the capacity that we have while healing and opening layer by layer once we give time and space to integrate it all. Sometimes we do this by ourselves and sometimes with the help of an expert. In between the ceremonies, it was life itself and my more open awareness of a huge part of my sexual trauma that had revealed itself. While deeply connecting with my body I sat and felt my belly. I was becoming miserable. I could feel a big topic coming up. 'Okay, you are safe, you are safe. Stay with it'. My own life energy had been conditioned as unsafe my whole life because it had been connected to the sexual abuse. So, when my life energy was flowing… I blocked it somewhere. Or I gave it away… I gave myself away. Many times. I didn't even know better. This was my conditioning. Wow!

Now, I can rewrite my story. I can reconnect with my life energy and feel that it's safe; feel that it's mine. A deep intimate connection with my life energy and all energy around me is one of the most beautiful teachings and I feel like a new life path has been born.

A life of joy and wonder

Nowadays, I feel so much wonder about life and everything that I can experience. There is so much magic. So much love, joy and pleasure all abundantly vibrating inside and around me. In the ayahuasca ceremonies I experience now, my journeys are way different than before. I've healed and opened up a lot already. Sometimes my system wants to dive deeper and deeper.

However, what ayahuasca is showing me is, 'You've already healed this part. It's okay, you don't have to go there.' This is a conditioning in my system to feel the urge to pull and dive into the deepest dungeons. While it can be helpful when it's needed, how amazing is it when it's not needed anymore? Instead of diving into creating and expanding, you can really start living and receiving yourself and life even more. Now I feel like this is coming to an end and I see 11:11 on my clock. Ha! Yes, this was a message of hope and guidance from the universe. Thank you.

The last thing I'd like to share with you is my 'secret' learned in my journey with plant medicine: Stay brave, curious, open-minded and away from expectations. Trust, surrender and let go. Play with the flow where the medicine and life take you. Choose love over fear – always. And remember, you are the medicine.

Much love and many blessings,
Myrthe de Jongh

About The Author

My name is Myrthe de Jongh. I was born on 04-04-1991 in a small village in the Netherlands, the country where I still live while living my royal sovereign truth.

I believe that one of my biggest life purposes on this earth is to live and learn love no matter how many life lessons are included. It's to help transform everything that is not love and to unleash our deepest, purest truth and (sexual) aliveness.

I've turned my life experiences, new knowledge from different studies, and deep remembrance and wisdom from my soul into my own business to guide other people on their journeys.

I don't like labels, but I call myself a 'sensual embodiment and integration guide with a Tantric approach'. I facilitate workshops, coaching programs, breathwork and plant medicine ceremonies. Such a gift!

I'd love to connect with and welcome you.
My website: www.myrthedejongh.com
Instagram: @myrthedejongh

Mindfulness through Addictions
By Niki Charlie

I grew up with a pretty wide understanding of the sacredness of life. As a child, I would watch my mother stand in reverence before nature's beauty. She taught me and my sisters about the abundance of the garden, the generosity of the forest, and the indefectible growth that we experience when we open our hearts to Her medicine. It took me years to embody those teachings and trust in the process of my ongoing healing journey.

I believe my birth was my first encounter with the shadows; my first mystical experience. It's one that I've taken the time to reflect upon for many years. I was born early; forced out of the womb. I wasn't ready. The umbilical cord was around my neck and my head was up. Thanks to modern medicine I am here today, but the idea that even as an unborn child, something in me wasn't ready to be birthed, got me thinking about my sense of belonging in this world.

I was so afraid growing up. My father was gone ninety percent of the time and I was an only child for ten years before my sisters were born, from another father. I didn't have much of a masculine presence to comfort me; to make me feel safe. My mother and I lived in remote places and would move to a new home almost yearly. "Our garden is our home," she would say. She was on her own quest. We didn't really have neighbours or community, we never really fit in, except amongst the trees, rivers, and mountains. We were nomads. We were always free, different, wild.

I developed hypervigilance and self-awareness at a very young age. I felt quite sad, and I realized later in life that I was in an almost constant state of depression. On the outside I was a sweet girl, always behaving. I did not speak much, nor did I voice my needs. I simply couldn't. I was petrified. However, I remember being six years old and thinking, "One day, I'll be happy."

When it comes to intergenerational trauma there is so much to address, so much to feel, and an incredible amount of work to do, and perhaps a lifetime isn't enough to finish it. However, it's enough to go through many, many transformations. The father wound was always first on my healing list. As far back as I could remember, I had been struggling with a lack of support, touch, and connection with my dad. He was perpetuating his own abandonment. I would cry myself to sleep for many years.

The hardship that came with my family line revealed itself over time, and as I transformed and learned new coping mechanisms, I also learned about the wounded masculine. The lack of support I was experiencing in my body came from many generations before me. I felt the needs of my ancestors not being met. I felt their pain in my chest, their closeness in my throat, and all their suppressed emotions in my belly.

The past is a story we tell ourselves. Over the years, I learned to slowly rewrite my story, dealing with the fears and learning to parent myself. I realized that I didn't have to carry around the past and that I could learn to free myself from it, slowly and with gratitude. I learned that I could lovingly nurture both the masculine and feminine aspects of myself and create my own sense of safety, and my own sense of belonging. I had to take responsibility for myself.

The blessings and breakthroughs that have happened so far in my life are the results of many years of addictions and heartbreaks, trial and error, and a combination of the teachings that sacred medicines helped me gain along the way. This is my imperfect journey to recovery.

Coming out of the cocoon

I was barely 15 when I tried MDMA for the first time. I can't say it was done properly; it was in the back of a car, late at night. A couple of older and unknown boys were driving my cousin and me. We didn't sleep that night. I had my first trip in my cousin's room hiding in the dark. It was definitely a transcendental experience. I remember the laughter. I remember the release and all my body's sensations. My cousin's face melting into the pillow. The tingling, aliveness of ecstasy. Rebellion. I didn't know anything about drugs. I surely didn't know that I would learn to self-medicate for years to come.

After that event, I spent over a decade using multiple drugs weekly. There were no distinctions between them. I didn't know how much was too much. The comedowns were so hard. It was its own kind of mutilation. Weakness. Depleted of vital force. There was a lot of mixing. Alcohol was my drug of choice, and I would top it up with anything that was available at that moment. Did it even matter what it was? I was silently experiencing complete made-up bliss states.

I was able to socialize. I felt in control. I was able to flirt and dance and laugh in front of people. My social anxiety was forgotten. I could let go of the wall I had built around myself. I could live my life "normally." It truly felt magical at times. As Gabor Maté puts it, "We need to ask addicts what is right with their addictions, not what is not working." What was right about suppressing all these emotions and not allowing myself to fully be in my body was the comfort of it all. The idea of not knowing, the avoidance of the pain. It was much easier to look away.

Shedding

I was 23 when I attempted suicide. I had been in a self-harm loop for many years at that point, had major eating disorders, and incessant self-criticism. It was Christmas Eve, and I was thousands of kilometers away from home — another one of my patterns was to move from place to place several times a year. I was so intoxicated with alcohol and cocaine that night that I didn't ask myself if eating 10 grams of mushrooms would be too much. I had never ingested that much. I was experimenting, learning on my own.

The mushrooms never lie. They took me exactly where I needed to go. My entire being went into decay that night, oblivion, total darkness. I thought to myself, "I have no more reasons to live." It was so clear and so obvious that something within me needed to die. I didn't know how to carry on and the setting wasn't right. I needed guidance but hadn't been taught how to ask for it.

I cut open my wrists, went into the bathtub to bleed, and prayed as intensely as I knew how while dragging myself to my bed to finally lose consciousness. A friend saved my life that night by calling the police. I ended up in the psychiatric hospital with 150 staples in my forearms. I had to fly back home. I needed a major reset.

When life sits you down in that way, there's no other choice but to reflect on it. So, I did for a while. Cannabis was my ally during that time. I would find myself painting all night until the sun rose, smoking and reflecting upon different times of my life. I connected with my dreams for the first time. The cycle I was in wasn't an easy one to break, but I knew I had started to shift internally. I felt different.

A year after that event, a boy I had been dating for a few months had a tragic bicycle accident on my birthday and died. I have to say, everything in my world shifted after that. I was seeing death from another perspective for the first time. It took me a long time to get myself back together and to be able to move through life normally again. I could feel his spirit everywhere. I was in shock. I was so attached to him and didn't know where to direct the love I had for him. I didn't know I needed that very same love to nurture my broken heart. I was simultaneously grieving him and rebirthing myself, perhaps for the first time ever. At that point, it was one of the most difficult things life had ever asked me to do. But grief saved me somehow. It made me want to live.

Adhikara

There's no linear order to what happened next. I just kept opening doors. I began a quest that was fulfilling in terms of knowledge, yet deeply confusing since I still had many issues I needed to work on. I began studying holistic health, yoga, ancient scriptures, indigenous wisdom and anything that was related to other forms of consciousness. The root cause of my issues started to reveal itself.

Why was I experiencing the same trauma over and over again? The sense of loss. The self-loathing. The omnipresent feeling of abandonment in my body. I was still terrified but growing. I still felt lonely but with a sense of purpose. The duality in my mind slowly started to fade away as I understood my place in the universe. The interconnectedness with every being and every particle.

I would gain more clarity when taking certain substances, mixed with daily yoga practice, meditation, and silence. I really started being more aware of what needed to change. I slowly trained myself to become the person I really wanted to be, and I knew it wouldn't just happen. I would have to be more conscious of certain aspects of my life. I needed to forgive myself and my ancestors. I would have to reconnect with my true self, with nature.

I eagerly dove into herbalism. The connection with Mother Earth put me on a path that was already true to my heart. I could see my inner child healing as I followed the seasons, as I watched plants grow from seeds to fruits, from roots to decay. I allowed my mind and psyche to absorb information that seemed lost in modern society. I wanted to fill the gap and remember what it is to be human upon the Earth. I reconnected with the ancient arts and truly started living my life as a ritual. Everything would be done with presence, care and love. My drug consumption wasn't as frequent, or at least was done with more consciousness, and more respect. I was healing, one day at a time, through reciprocity with nature.

As I slowly shed things from the past, other struggles resurfaced. The transition to becoming a woman was a complex one. I was looking for my tribe, for my essence. The last summer of my twenties, I spent lots of time in the ocean, feeling the water as medicine on my body. Something was also seeking me, but I wasn't necessarily making myself available to receive it.

Opening my heart

I remember this one night in Tofino, I sat down with these two guys I had just met, and they reintroduced me to MDMA. They shared their stories, telling me where the drug came from and how much they usually take. They asked me what kind of experience I was looking for; what I was fearing the most. They listened. It was a ceremony. We spent the night connecting and falling in love with the sounds, with the movements of our bodies caressing one another. I still have a vision of the two of them kneeling in front of me as I was dancing naked, feeling the magical energy of the goddess in and around me. My heart was shining out as I was inviting all the softness to transport me into a new reality. I had never felt so inherently free. It felt safe, awkward and real.

A couple of days later, I met a woman who would change my life forever. She was the mirror to my soul; the friend I had been waiting for my entire life. The one who would hold space for me for years to come. We shared a moment under the full moon, howling at the sky, taking deep breaths of release. An unimaginable amount of juicy love invaded every part of me. It was my initiation to womanhood and true friendship.

The next day, I fractured my ankle, perhaps intentionally. Another starting point. A call for deep rest. Life once again sent me back home, asking me to fully stop, to integrate. So much had happened. I had to relearn to walk, both physically and emotionally. It was a long convalescence, and I took great care during it.

Around the same time, I began taking an interest in microdosing on psilocybin. I humbly reopened the door to the mushroom world, and an interest in Ayahuasca was sparked. I decided I was going to prepare myself to undertake a journey with Her, when the time came. I kept a diary and wrote down my intentions and my dreams, and saw the progress. I was lovingly walking myself back home.

These events taught me to open up in a more delicate way. Like a flower, petal by petal, I would let others see my vulnerability while learning to ask for help. I created a home in my heart, and I got into a relationship that allowed me to be seen and in which I could learn to nurture my inner garden and invite many forms of healing along the way.

Cycles

By the age of 34, I had been microdosing for a couple of years, as well as tracking my moon cycle as a way to navigate my emotions. It helped me realize that the idea of growth is never over. There are many fluctuations and it's okay. For even life itself goes dormant, back down into the roots, and into the womb of the world. Embodying the Earth, like mycelium, we can learn to evolve with grace and use it as a way to elevate ourselves into the light, reaching for the sun, mimicking the cyclical aspects of life and constantly transforming.

I have been on a quest for beauty and expansion since birth, following an inner call for authenticity. I am giving myself time, bathing in streams and listening to the beating of my heart. I broke down and rebuilt myself again and again. I wouldn't be here today if it wasn't for all the people who supported me along the way, and if I hadn't had the courage to witness my own death many times, and to make peace with the darkest parts of me. Now I know that life prepared me for it, even before I was born. I learn through experience, connection, and depth.

It hasn't been an easy path, but it is a rewarding one. And I know it's not over. I know that all this preparation is slowly giving me the force to support others on their journey, as I am supporting my own. I know that I have much more to learn and that life will take me places I am least expecting. I know now that my soul's calling is to live in harmony and to slow down in order to feel more.

There is hope.

About The Author

Niki Charlie is originally from Quebec City, Canada. She is a holistic chef, yoga teacher and soul explorer, but above all, she is a lifelong student.

Niki is a consistently and continuously expanding soul who likes all things comfortable, and she understands this life through a spiritual scope. This vivid curiosity about the human experience has led her to explore the path of the healing arts, nutrition, plant medicine, femininity, intimacy, communication, and magic.

These interests are tied together by Nature Herself and have been an immense source of support, wisdom and inspiration throughout her life. Niki's creations honor Mother Earth's cycles, versatility, diversity, inclusivity and balance in one way or another.

Niki knows and recognizes the complexities that constitute the human experience, and she dedicates much of her life to connecting with herself and others to bring healing into this world.

Get in touch with Niki by sending an email to: info.earthyniki@gmail.com or connecting with her on Instagram at: @earthy.niki

12
Return with Elixir

The Return with the Elixir phase in the Hero's Journey is a stage where the hero returns to their ordinary world, bringing back the treasure or knowledge they have gained on their journey. It is a moment of integration and transformation, as the hero uses their newfound knowledge and abilities to make a positive impact on their community.

Similarly, taking psychedelics or entering shamanic ceremonies can also lead to a moment of transformation and integration, where individuals bring back the insights and wisdom gained from their experience to their daily life. This can lead to a greater sense of purpose and meaning, as individuals use their newfound understanding to make a positive impact on the world around them.

The experience of returning with the elixir can also lead to a greater sense of connection with others, as individuals use their experiences to build relationships and connections with others who have undergone similar journeys. This can lead to the formation of communities and networks that are focused on personal growth, healing, and transformation.

Additionally, the experience of returning with the elixir can be a moment of empowerment and self-realization. By confronting and overcoming their deepest fears and obstacles, individuals may gain a greater sense of self-awareness and self-confidence, allowing them to live a more authentic and fulfilling life.

However, it's important to note that the experience of returning with the elixir can also be challenging, as individuals may struggle to integrate their experiences into their daily lives. They may need to find ways to communicate their insights and wisdom to others, or to find a new sense of purpose and direction.

Ultimately, the experience of returning with the elixir can be a powerful reminder of the transformative potential of altered states of consciousness, and of the importance of using our experiences and knowledge to make a positive impact on the world around us.

In our first story by Dr. Aimee Callahan, we see how a powerful death/rebirth experience can bring forth a new sense of purpose in life. After being hunted and almost killed in a horrific attack by her daughter's father, Aimee suffered from PTSD. She tried a pharmacy of pills to cope but only experienced relief after she found psilocybin.

The second story by American author Dr. Jill Stocker is a mix of personal revelations and lessons that she's taking forward in life thanks to sacred medicine. Sacred medicine helped Jill to listen to her body's messages. Her emotional and physical womb trauma (the result of terrible abuse) was healed. She believes that women everywhere need to tap into their divine inner wisdom to be able to heal themselves and the world.

The third story in this chapter by American author Gregg Westwood shows that the elixir we return with can be as close as our own breath, our voice. Traumatized as a child by an insensitive teacher, Gregg carried the wounds in his psyche for almost 60 years. He embarked on a sacred journey to Ecuador to meet Grandmother Ayahuasca. He flew home, finally feeling grounded and at peace, ready to serve and heal others.

Finally, a heartfelt sharing by American author Sandra Dee Nicholson, shows us the power of freedom we gain when we can finally face our shadow with courage. Sandra Dee has been a criminal for over 40 years. Yet...her use of illegal marijuana as a medicine has brought her peace and healing. Her story, and personal apology to marijuana, lifts the veil of ignorance covering the use of this herb.

Dying to be Reborn:
Breaking the Bonds of PTSD with Psilocybin
By Aimee Callahan

The night I almost died went something like this.

Somewhere in my sleepy haze, I awoke to an earth-shattering boom and the cracking sounds of wood breaking. A large man dressed in all black was kicking in the front door of my shabby little college rental house.

Boom! Crack! I was immediately frozen with fear. The man in black suddenly standing over me in my bed was Death staring me in the face. He had a terrifying look of unshaking determination completely void of relatable human emotion. As the man pulled me out of my bed and dragged me into the living room, my fingernails ripped off into the wall and left a bloody trail. The man in black had one clear message for me, "I'm going to slit your throat from ear to ear and I'm not leaving until you're dead."

My adrenaline rushed so intensely that I struggled to breathe through my panic. I felt like I was having a heart attack. My body began to shiver uncontrollably. The moment that would determine my fate had arrived. I had a decision to make. I was a broke, full-time graduate student and single mom sharing a bed with my two-year-old child. I was her sole emotional and financial provider. I needed to protect her, too. It was time for me to choose to fight to protect us or die.

My mind was spinning. Utter terror took hold of me as I immediately realized how helpless I was. I was a flimsy little ragdoll in his hands. He was much larger and stronger than me. He threw me around in a way that let me know he was in total control of me.

Overwhelmed with terror and deep remorse, the depth of which I cannot describe, I realized at that moment this is how my life would end. I was facing a horrible, violent death. Until this moment I was a little deer in the headlights. I don't know how to fight! How could I possibly fight off this strong man? But I knew I didn't have a choice.

As my adrenaline slowed a bit, it became like a magic serum feeding instantaneous thoughts of survival to my brain. Images of the impending reality of someone finding my little girl next to my bloody body went through my mind. What would happen to her if I died? I pictured my family planning my funeral. Anger bubbled up in me at the injustice of this moment. No one has the right to take away my life and my right to raise my child. I was ready to fight to the death.

My precious Daughter

My little girl helped save my life. She is a heavy sleeper and had slept through the mayhem up to the point he had me pinned down on the couch. At that moment, my daughter walked toward the living room, sleepy and confused, dressed in her tiny pink pajamas with dainty flowers, innocently asking, "Mommy?" My heart sank. I didn't want her to see me die, especially in such a horrible way. I calmly begged him, "Please put her in the bedroom so she won't have to watch?" I felt an indescribable sense of relief when I saw him get off me to put her back in the bedroom. She would hear what would happen, but at least she would not see it.

I saw my escape. I was no longer pinned to the couch. I sprang up, jumped over the ottoman, and ran into the kitchen where I had a large can of bear spray on the top of the refrigerator. Living in Wyoming at the time, I hiked often and always had bear spray with me. He was on me immediately. I turned around and sprayed him directly in his eyes from less than 2 inches away. I kept my finger pressed on the bear spray trigger and thought to myself, "I don't care if I get sprayed too. I will fumigate this cockroach". Soon we were both covered in pepper spray. It hung in the air like a toxic, gray mist. The pepper spray did not slow him down, it only made him more angry.

While fighting for my life, I was screaming at the top of my lungs to try and get my neighbors to hear. He immediately tackled me to the kitchen floor where I banged my heels on the floor as loudly as I could to try and wake up my downstairs neighbors.

I had experienced many stalking events with this individual and when I'd moved into that particular house, I'd made sure there was a family in the basement who could hear if something ever went wrong. That precaution helped save my life.

The next thing I knew, he wrestled the bear spray away from me and suddenly he had me held in a reverse choke hold. My feet were hanging above the floor. I was going to die from him choking me to death. He had won. I lost my ability to breathe and knew at that moment that this was how my life would end. My legs kicked furiously but as I lost oxygen they slowed to a flutter. I could feel my life being choked out of me moment by moment. This man was willing to stop at nothing, to go to prison or worse, just to see me dead.

The man in black who had broken into our home to murder me was my daughter's father. It had been a moment I'd feared for a long time and my intuition kept telling me that what was happening was inevitable. I'd known that this man would come after me one day. I'd known that if he didn't get what he wanted, he would try to kill me.

As my life was being choked out of my body, I felt unbelievable anguish over losing my life in such a violent, horrible manner. How did I end up here? I used to be a free-spirited girl who was full of dreams who used to believe she could do anything. What had happened to the girl who'd traveled the world and backpacked foreign countries solo? Even to this day, as hard as I try to find the words, I simply cannot begin to describe the sense of deep, dark despair I felt while dying.

Saved!

Then, a miracle happened. A police officer burst in and yelled at my attacker to let me go. I made it outside safely. I was in pure shock and standing on my front porch in my underwear screaming at the top of my lungs covered in bear spray with my eyes swollen shut. This was an out-of-body experience for me. I could hear someone screaming from a distance and knew it was me, but I could not connect with being able to stop screaming in terror at that moment. I was somewhere else entirely.

What I remember next is hearing the police take my attacker out of the house past me to the police car. My downstairs neighbors had called the police the moment they'd heard the door being busted in. The police found my little girl trembling and staring into space with her mouth open in terror. They wrapped her in a blanket and gave her a teddy bear. They put me in the front seat of a warm police car and put her in my arms. I sobbed with relief and rocked her tightly. We had gone through absolute hell, but we were ALIVE.

As for that adventurous, independent girl I once knew who backpacked solo overseas? Well, she was still here, but I wouldn't see her again for many years to come. Although my attacker went to prison, my sense of safety disappeared. To this day, I cannot sleep alone in a ground-level house. We live in a high-rise apartment in the center of the city with 24/7 security. I feel safe living in the sky.

Pain, pills, and alcohol

That night is not how my story ends. In many ways, it's how it begins. The journey ahead would not be easy, but through psilocybin journeys I learned to embrace my pain and transmute it into purpose.

The onset of PTSD was life-shattering. Although I felt immense gratitude to be alive, immediately after my fight for survival, PTSD began to take hold of my mind, body, and soul. When my therapist first informed me that I had "acute stress" I jokingly told her, "There is nothing cute about it!" Even in the darkest moments I still have my offbeat sense of humor.

For weeks after the attack, I heard the sounds of my screaming in my head. Whether I was teaching my class at the local community college or playing with my daughter, my screams haunted me. I relived the attempted murder every night in my dreams for the next two years. The moment I would start to hit deep dream sleep, my mind would revert to caveman mode to wake me up to relive the terrifying moment the man in black was standing over me in bed.

PTSD is like living in a nightmare loop that replays again and again and can be easily triggered by normal, everyday occurrences.

Every time I heard a door slam or loud noise, I was immediately transported back into a full adrenaline "fight or flight" mode. My PTSD triggers hijacked my life regularly. I tried everything within my reach to cope and numb the pain. I was seriously sleep-deprived and desperate for relief.

To help me cope with PTSD during the day, I went through a smorgasbord of anti-anxiety medications. Most pills left me feeling foggy until I tried Lexapro, a selective serotonin reuptake inhibitor (SSRI) used to treat depression and generalized anxiety disorder (GAD). Soon Lexapro and I had formed a bond that would last many years.

Sleeping pills were prescribed to me like candy. I tried nearly every pill on the market to help me sleep at night. I was ready to sell my soul to stop the PTSD loop of reliving the attack nightly in my dreams. Not one sleeping pill worked. Finally, I began to self-medicate with what did work. After I'd put my daughter to sleep, I would drink wine until I was numb enough to fall asleep. Within a short period of time, what started as one glass would turn into many more. I knew I was falling into a vicious cycle of self-medicating my pain. For the first time in my life, I understood that trauma and addiction are two sides of the same coin.

Late one night after drinking too much wine and exhausted from sleep deprivation, I fell asleep in the bathtub while the water was running. I miraculously woke up as my head began to submerge. The bathroom was completely flooded with half a foot of water. I should have drowned. My guardian angels were busy that night. This was the final turning point for me to stop coping and start healing as if my life depended upon it, because it did. I hadn't survived an attempted murder to end up killing myself. That was not how I wanted my story to end.

Relief at last

I turned to psilocybin because I had nowhere left to turn. I live in Denver, Colorado, USA where psilocybin is decriminalized for personal use. Discussions about the benefits of psilocybin are common here among local Denverites. I quickly learned that psilocybin is not a party drug or something to be scared of. It is a sacred, ceremonial plant medicine that works to slow down the hyperactive panic center in our brain and creates an information superhighway that promotes full somatic healing.

Also known as the amygdala, our lizard brain works to keep us safe. Our amygdala means well, it just hasn't evolved much since we lived in caves. Every time my PTSD was triggered, my amygdala worked to keep me in "fight or flight" mode as if I was still living in a cave and needed my adrenaline rush to run from a saber tooth tiger.

I refer to psilocybin as Pachamama, the "mother earth" goddess revered by the indigenous peoples of the Andes. Considered holy sacraments, the Aztecs referred to mushrooms as "flesh of the gods". Pachamama is wise. She has been around since the dawn of plants on earth and has been used in ceremonies for thousands of years. She will only reveal to you what you need to know. She will not let you abuse her as she is not addictive. She is to be loved, honored and respected and in return, she offers the gift of life-altering insight and transformational healing.

My psilocybin journey began with microdosing. A microdose is not intoxicating, but its effects are powerful. Within days, my brain ceased reacting to my usual PTSD triggers. I began sleeping through the night. I was not numb but fully present. For the first time since the attack, I did not experience panic attacks. My goofy sense of

247

humor quickly returned. Colors were a bit brighter. Flowers smelled more beautiful. Sex became hyper-sensory. Food tasted better. My creative energy flowed once again. I reconnected with the girl who had once traveled the world solo.

The first time I experienced ego loss during a psilocybin ceremony, I experienced incredible breakthroughs. My therapist and I integrated all that was revealed to me during the ceremony for the next six months. The effects of psilocybin on releasing my trauma and regaining my joy in life have been remarkable. As I mindfully process all that Pachamama offers me, I now microdose and sit in ceremony only when needed.

I have learned from my psilocybin journey that it does not take much for this sacred medicine to help the healing process. Psilocybin is not a silver bullet, but it packs a lot of silver. To maximize my psilocybin healing journey, I did not expect Pachamama to do all of the work. I consciously doubled down on meditation, prayer, journaling, and trauma therapy. Lexapro helped me cope, but it could not help me heal. Within a year of my psilocybin healing journey, I had slowly weaned myself off of Lexapro and any desire to misuse alcohol completely disappeared.

Turning pain into purpose

Eventually, I went on to write my first book, *The Re-Wilding of Womxn: Release Your Inner Wild to Live the Life of Your Dreams*. I created a Top 50 podcast, Now and Zen, my passion project to share the neuroscience of joy with listeners worldwide. Psilocybin also empowered me to finally let go of my anger. I learned to forgive someone who is not sorry for trying to kill me. My forgiveness does not erase the past, but it allows me to reflect upon it with compassion for what I survived.

I learned so much from almost dying. There is a saying, "Don't waste your pain; use it to help others." Although I am still a work in progress, my survival experience became a higher calling for me. Helping others helps me heal. Having been released from that dark place, I dedicate my life to spreading the gift of joy in the world, because we all deserve to feel the beauty of life! My daughter has grown into a healthy, well-adjusted teenager and an honor student with a bright future. If my story of survival and journey of healing can help even one person, then my goal of sharing it is complete.

About The Author

Dr. Aimee Callahan (Ed.D.) is the Amazon Best Selling Author of *The Re-Wilding of Womxn: Release Your Inner Wild to Live the Life of Your Dreams*. She is the creator and host of Now and Zen, a Top 50 podcast, created to share the neuroscience of joy with the world. She is an expert on the neuroscience of adult learning, a speaker, a spiritual gangster, a lazy but avid meditator, and a fellow trauma survivor. Aimee's mission is to help others on their spiritual and trauma-healing journeys through the neuroscience of mindfulness.

Aimee has worked as a leader in higher education for over 20 years and regularly hosts ceremonies and workshops in her hometown of Denver, Colorado, USA. When she is not writing, speaking or hosting kick-ass events, you can find her riding her motorcycle with her fellow wind sisters or walking her dachshund in the park.

Visit Aimee online: www.draimeecallahan.com

Learning to Live from My Womb, Not My Wound
By Jill Stocker, DO

I felt it immediately in my clitoris, the part I had been so disconnected from and "dead inside". It was a burning, a wildfire, then a pulsating energy that pumped full body orgasm wave of pleasure and awakening throughout my being. I was overtaken by it and fully surrendered to it…writhing and moaning endlessly.

This was only my second experience with sacred plant medicine. My first experience with ayahuasca, two years prior, had cracked me wide open to the sacred wisdom of not only the medicine but also helped unlock the innate wisdom deep within my body, more specifically, in my womb.

My journey back home to myself began in January 2019. I had what I thought was a sinus infection for a month. And that, too, had started with a pulsating energy…but I hadn't known how to listen to my body's inherent wisdom yet. So, I did what I, like most Western medicine people, had been taught…medicated it. I did this for several weeks, medicating to be functional enough to work, then collapsing into a puddle for the remainder of the day/night.

One day, I remembered hearing a woman talking about listening to her body's messages…so I called her. Her question after listening to me was, what if I, rather than trying to silence this very frantic part of me, talked to it, asked it what it had to say or what it needed? Hmmm, an interesting concept I'd never heard of or practiced before. So, into the bath (my safe "womb" space) I went!

I asked this burning area between my eyes what it was trying to say and what it needed. There was an almost instantaneous melting

251

of the fire between my eyes. It had been demanding my attention all along and I had kept saying, "I feel like my third eye is on fire," but I hadn't been truly listening to my body's messages. Lesson: Investigation and self-education over medication.

The invitation, the call

A few weeks later, I received a dear friend's invitation to attend her first sacred plant medicine retreat, specifically, Grandmother Ayahuasca. Without hesitation, my body said, YES! My reason for going, I thought, was to find my purpose in humanity. I was at a crossroads with my career and wanting more, knowing I was meant for more and needing to ascend out of my current situation. I couldn't see the path, the staircase, or even the next step…I just knew there was MORE I was supposed to do and be. And while I did get this clarity with the medicine… as they say, "The medicine doesn't give you what you want, it gives you what you need" (even that which you may be completely unaware of, which was the case for me).

Revealing hidden trauma

While many people purge in the form of vomiting during ayahuasca ceremonies, my release was literally to "give birth" to my massive unhealed womb trauma I'd had no idea was there. (It had been caused by early childhood sexual abuse/molestation, sexual abuse in romantic relationships, including coercion and trafficking, and the birth of my children). Locked deep within was also my divine femininity, my power, and ultimately my true essence. What I was shown by the medicine was not just the trauma of my own birth as an infant, but also the incredible amount of trauma my womb and the rest of my body had been carrying since having my children – all three C-sections.

My firstborn had been an emergency, as she'd had the umbilical cord wrapped around her neck three times. For both of us to survive, we'd had to be ripped apart, literally. Not only had I not seen her when they'd taken her out, but they had then put me in a room alone for several hours. Later, when they'd wheeled her bassinet in, I'd thought to myself, is that my baby? Talk about complete dissociation from my body, my feelings, my baby, and ultimately, myself! I hadn't shed one tear during the entire process; my body had simply done what it had needed to do to survive such massive trauma. It had shut down to protect me.

This happened again with the birth of my second child, when I almost died. There was a repeat of my baby being taken away from me and my being put away in a room alone for hours. No tears, no NOTHING, complete shutdown.

It took the sacred wisdom of the plant medicine for me to be able to see all of this trauma I'd been carrying around/storing in my womb for almost two decades! My hips were incredibly tight at the start of the ceremony, as if my body was holding on for dear life. By the end of the ceremony, I had "birthed" all that stored pain and dissociation and finally had full, fluid movement in my pelvic area. Then what? I had purged the pain, but I had no idea how to BE in my body then. That would come the next night and in the following years as I integrated more.

After the release came more information: trapped within all that pain in my womb from the births and sexual abuse/trauma was my direct connection to myself, my true essence, my divine feminine, my power, my creativity, my inherent wisdom, safety,

253

security (physical, emotional, mental, sexual, financial) — soooo much!!!

This first experience allowed a lot to be purged, so that subsequent experiences could instill/infuse more sacred medicine wisdom into me, or rather, reconnect me with my own body's inherent wisdom and its eternal connection with the universal wisdom – Gaia. I needed to be cleansed to be able to be filled, to be able to be ready to see more and go deeper.

Disconnect to connect

Sacred plant medicine allows me to unplug from my very strong Default Mode Network, stored brain patterns of all that I've learned in life so far. It's material that ultimately needs to be unlearned to restore me to my true essence and innocence. It allows me to connect with my highest self, the energy of the Universe, the vibration of pure love and acceptance of what is. It connects me to my true divine essence, who I was before all the stories and limiting beliefs got encoded in my brain and body. It helps me get past the fears and coping mechanisms, and allows me to see the pure potentiality of me, of all, fearlessness, limitlessness, and connection to all regardless of space and time.

The divine in me can recognize the divine in you and all beings. The medicine journeys help restore us to oneness, bliss, and the reality that we are all one humanity. It shows me my role in the Universe.

Lessons from the medicine

Can you imagine seeing music and hearing colors? Feeling the music of YOU? This is what happened for me when I followed my inner calling toward sacred ceremonies…but this was just part of my process of discovering my WILD.

Let me tell you about one night in the jungle. I used to be afraid of the dark…until I received a message from the fireflies in the jungle during an ayahuasca ceremony. What if you were called to be your own light source so you could see in the dark? What if the dark was just as beautiful and not scary at all? And what about all the many shades in between? Too often we think of love and light and carefree-ness as the only beauty or desired feeling. But what if it's ALL part of the magic of you and you can embrace ALL of it? What if you could start every day with "Who am I today?", "Who do I want to be today?", "What are you longing for today?"

For years I had a deep longing inside…nothing seemed to fill it. It turns out this deep longing I was feeling was for myself, for all my light, dark, and my wild.

What if you could just feel all of your feelings and not try to make something magical out of them all the time? What if instead of trying to make your shit sparkle, you just fully embraced the vastness of the emotions flowing wildly through you?

I have come to understand that my ability to feel it all is also my ability to heal it all, as well as my ability and capacity to love unconditionally. I was BORN for this role. I had to face all these things to BECOME the healer I always needed, to then help others heal themselves.

"Your conflicts, all the difficult things, the problematic situations in your life are not chance or haphazard. They are specifically yours, designed specifically for you by a part of you that loves you more than anything else. That part of you that loves you more than anything else has created roadblocks to lead you to your self."

~ A.H. Almaas

My purpose and mission

I now know, my body KNOWS, when it needs more wisdom to go deeper, farther, into the healing and ultimately raising the vibration of myself, the collective consciousness, the collective divine feminine revolution that is so direly needed not just to heal, but also to transcend the current state of the world. Women are portals between worlds and tapping into the ancient divine inner wisdom of their own portal (whether they've given birth or not) is what is so desperately needed. Heal yourself, heal the world. Heal your womb, heal many worlds.

The purpose in humanity I was searching for has revealed itself to me through various sacred medicine insights, as well as my inner wisdom finally being able to reveal itself. My purpose is to be a healing vessel to help others heal so that they may be liberated from their wounds and live and move freely in their bodies, and to aid in the healing of the divine feminine within all (men and women), ultimately helping reclaim their inner power, personal safety and security, body and sacred sexual, womb sovereignty, moving from victim to warrior, to then help with healing of the collective.

Many life experiences, outside influences, and traumas — individual, generational, and collective — can influence and impact a person's ability to be fully in their power and sovereignty. Reconnecting with a person's *wild* through various modalities (breathwork, dance, embodiment, and somatic experience practices, and more) can help clear shame, trauma, and low vibrational energy, so you can lead a more fulfilled connection with yourself, feeling lighter, freer, and more creative. You can FLOW (finances too!) with an enhanced sense of vibrancy and inner vitality, and ultimately...LIBERATION!

In the immersive experience of working together with men and women from all backgrounds, I serve as the healing vessel to explore what your soul is craving. Womb trauma is not just limited to women (it can affect men too!). It can span from the trauma you may have suffered in the womb, during your own childbirth or in your lineage, sexual trauma/ancestral sexual trauma, miscarriages/abortions.

Takeaways so far from working with sacred medicine

I have had to become the healer I needed, because there was no one healer or modality that had all that I needed and hungered for. In doing this, I've found the below realizations for myself, that I know now I'm meant to share with others traveling on a similar path.

Sacred medicine has brought me:

- Enhanced connection to and anchoring in my Feminine Self and power, as well as integration of my own Divine Masculine and Feminine, being a safe container for myself first, then others

- Clarity of how and who I wish to embody and move forward in the world, fully expressed and empowered

- Tools to connect with my parts on my own and move from living and expressing from my womb, not my wound

- The ability to access and feel the full spectrum of joy, vitality, health, creative expression, safety, security, power, and sovereignty, to go from surviving to thriving

Tools and mantras I've found helpful on my journeys

LISTEN

L Look Within

I Investigate (old narratives, limiting beliefs, fears)

S Still Yourself

T Tell Someone Safe (we heal in relationship and need help integrating)

E Engage (your inner healer to speak up and out for what they need, and your outer healers for additional support if needed for integration to the fully realized YOU)

N Narrate your new story of YOU!

What's coming is going

All the random thoughts/memories that are coming up from your past are being released from your cells/body, to be purged/cleansed from your system...allow this and say, "Thank you" when it's releasing.

Let go

Let go of all limiting beliefs and stories you may have been told or told yourself of how you or your life should look. Let go of outcomes, let go of what you know...there is something even more magical and powerful, a higher knowing to surrender to.

Heal...at ALL costs

Investing in your healing journey with different modalities is a radical and courageous act that most people don't do...you deserve it, and you can't afford NOT to heal at ALL costs.

Original poems inspired by sacred medicine

The In Between
The moment you let go of one trapeze to fully grip the next
The moment you catch your breath
The moment you release the old version and hold the hand of
the new version.
But it's not take one hat off and put on another...
There's an "in between"
A grief for what was, and a trepidation for what will be
Can you sit in the in-between and just listen
To the beat of your own heart,
The hum of your own soul,
The Beingness of YOU

It's You
What if you could feel your inner pulsating and see the colors
of you?
What if you felt trapped in your body and couldn't move to
the music you were hearing and feeling...or could you?
But you weren't. Why? Judgement?
What if the whole world was waiting for you to dance or sing
or be the most fabulous you?
You're the one you've been waiting for, searching for...

So live.
And dance.
And feel it all.
Become one with nature...and this experience.

Float with the waves some moments.

And others, ride them—even when oceans fall from your eyes.

As you watch the flicker of a flame, become the fire and light up the sky so that no darkness can survive.

Become one with the earth and melt into oneness.

Love her.

Love you.

Love all the parts of you.

You are her…and she is you, infinitely.

What will happen when there's no more longing?

When there's nothing missing?

You're whole.

You've arrived at you…the home that was always within.

JOY

Just for a moment

Oh elusive one

You thrill me when you're here, and leave me wanting more of your magic carpet ride,

Wondering how to capture whatever magic formula that caused you to appear.

Oh, how I'd love to capture you and bottle you up, to access at all times…

But perhaps that's the magic of you…

Would I appreciate you as much if you were always there?

Would I be able to recognize the heights I soar to with you if we were always flying at the same level?

I'll enjoy each dance with you and anxiously, breathlessly, await the next one…and learn to enjoy the moments in between dances.

About The Author

Dr. Jill Stocker is traditionally trained and board-certified in family medicine, with advanced certification in age management medicine and hormone optimization. She focuses on the whole person—physically, mentally, emotionally, spiritually and sexually. Her professional, evidence-based training combined with her personal and life experiences, intuitive gifts and commitment to helping others fully awaken and thrive in all areas of their lives make for a transformational experience for her patients. She has also added psychedelic medicine (particularly ketamine-assisted psychotherapy) and trauma-informed medicine to her practice to help her patients further expand into themselves and their lives. Her goal is to help change the medical and mental health care paradigm from numbers-oriented, medication-based sick care to individual-focused well care and liberation to the most realized version of self.

LA Magazine's Top Doctor, Forbes Health Advisory Board member. Located in Los Angeles, offering hormone optimization (men and women), psychedelic integration, Ketamine Assisted Psychotherapy, and Life Integration Transformation (LIT) sessions both in person and remotely, and hosts retreats worldwide starting fall 2023.

Learn more about Dr. Jill at www.drjillstocker.com

Surrendering to Spirit:
Releasing Shame to Embody Leadership
By Gregg Westwood

Like all of us, I was born with a divine light that was brilliant, uniquely creative, and innocent. As a young boy, I joyfully expressed my light through acting, singing, and dancing.

On one very bright sunny day, the little girls and boys of my kindergarten class restlessly gathered in a circle for a milk and cookies break. As I began to open my milk carton, I noticed that my teacher had approached me and was now hovering over me. I sensed something was terribly wrong. As I slowly lifted my gaze, I saw her disapproving glare, her left hand on her hip and her right finger pointing firmly at a puddle on the floor in front of me. She called out loudly, "What is that, Gregg?"

I had wet my pants.

Humiliated, I froze and every muscle became stiff as a wave of warmth flushed up my body from my toes to my face. My shoulders rose to my ears, as I gasped for air and stopped breathing. My heart pounded and all of my body's systems began shutting down. My jaw clenched, my lips pursed, my eyes crossed inside my head, and my mind went blank. I could sense everyone staring at me. Their silence was deafening. I frantically searched for what seemed like hours for the right words that would not expose me for what had just happened.

As my head dropped in shame, I saw my milk carton. "I spilled my milk," I said, staring at the floor. She retorted, "That is not milk." Of course, the puddle was not milk; it wasn't white. I shut my eyes, trying to become invisible, as I was carried away to change my wet pants.

My pathway to empowerment

My innocence had been stolen, and of course, this traumatic memory has lived in my body for almost 60 years. I have learned to comfort the shrinking shame that my inner child feels, but it wasn't until recently, when I embarked on a sacred journey to Ecuador, that I became aware of how deeply this freezing wound had stopped me from embodying my true self.

As I boarded my flight to Quito, Ecuador, I wondered what my sacred journey had in store for me. I felt that I was missing a skill as a healer. I heard that "Grandmother," what the indigenous people of South America call the plant medicine *ayahuasca*, didn't give you what you wanted. Instead, she always gave you what you needed. I soon discovered the truth of that statement.

The first two days of my journey, I met with each shaman individually. My first session was with a gentle man dressed in all white with a colorful headband and flowing black hair. As I meditated near the fire pit, he said that he saw a light shine down upon my head through the hole in the roof. He told me that I need to own my talents, respect their powers, and be grateful to the spirits for them. He already knew my issue of never quite allowing myself to embrace the power of my gifts.

This message was confirmed by the rest of the shamans who were women. One of them emphatically said, "You are ready, Gregorio. Your role is to hold people's hands as you guide them into their darkness. And when a healing has occurred, you will accompany each soul up and into the light of transcendence."

I always knew I was a healer. Even strangers have felt comfortable sharing their struggles with me. Being very sensitive, I could sense people's pain in my body like it was my own and I always felt compassion for them. I could see their light in their darkness. Growing up with alcoholic grandparents, positive examples of expressing darker emotions like sadness, anger, or any form of vulnerability were not modeled. So, I had to hide my true self to receive love. I turned to my world of theater and dance where I received applause for expressing my array of emotions in characters. But even in that safe container, I often feared being seen in the shame of that day in kindergarten. On stage, I even chose not to wear my contact lenses, because I performed best when I could not see the faces of the audience, thus avoiding possible humiliation.

The fourth day of my sacred journey consisted of a 10-hour sweat lodge accompanied by San Pedro medicine. After several rounds of drinking cups of the medicine and sweating, we were given rocks to cleanse and bless ourselves with. I felt drawn to rubbing mine, a black heart-shaped rock from the Rio Nupe, a headwater of the Amazon River, on my heart, solar plexus and my lower abdomen and genitals. Since it was so dark inside, I felt safe massaging and drawing circles with the rock on those areas of my body where I had shrunk, and which were in need of love. After the healing exercise was finished, I handed off the rock and it was carried out of the lodge to be blessed and released. I didn't realize at the time that this was the first step in the healing of my second chakra.

Freeing my silent voice

I had always felt my second chakra was contracted and shut down in the expression of my true creativity. It was as though my kindergarten humiliation had followed me. As a young therapist, I struggled with sharing my wisdom. One day, two traditional psychotherapists asked me to join them on a panel to talk about the benefits of body-centered therapy. Some of my students were in the audience and when seeing the expectation in their eyes, I froze. I had no words and I watched as their faces and glances turned away from me in embarrassment. My worst fear had come true. I was humiliated in front of the people I was supposedly leading.

From the pitch-black darkness, I heard the shaman's voice call out to me, "Gregorio, sing," and someone handed me a rattle. I froze just like I did as a kindergarten boy and as a young therapist. Who was I to lead a part of this sacred sweat lodge ceremony? Allowing the medicine of San Pedro to hold me, I took a deep breath, found the rhythm of the rattle, and began singing the song of the Eagle.

As I ventured into the world of San Pedro without my sight, my voice sounded like it was amplified, almost echoing into infinity in this cramped womb-like circle that suddenly felt spacious. I sang four rounds and during the second round, everyone joined in during the chorus. The shock of disbelief that this was happening turned to ecstatic joy as their voices sent chills down my spine and vibrated throughout my entire being.

As I left this sacred space of dirt and branches, I gave thanks to the sacred medicine that had given me the strength to embody my divine light and role of a leader, by allowing Spirit to move through me fully and freely.

Finally, meeting "Grandmother"

It was the final night of my journey when I was to meet Grandmother. As I entered the bamboo house, the smoky scents of palo santo and sage wafted through the candlelit room, and it glowed with sacred presence. The shaman, a woman with deep brown eyes and light brown skin, dressed in a flowing white tunic and pants with a navy-blue turban covering her hair, greeted me with a gentle nod and soft smile. Her altar, overflowing with flowers and sacred tools, was in the corner in front of me and there was one empty seat by itself next to it. I had to take it.

I approached the altar for my first cup of tea. She handed me the cup with sacred intention, and I drank the medicine with respect for what I was about to experience. I returned to my seat and within a few minutes I saw a kaleidoscope of vivid, bold colors and patterns, feathers, and jaguars that were definitely from South America. With my intention of growing as a healer, I opened my eyes to witness this healing ceremony.

Then something very heavy descended upon me. My head dropped and I felt dizzy and nauseous. Having had a lot of experience with throwing up both physically and energetically in ceremonies, in my personal work and work with clients, I knew this is what I must do to heal myself at the deepest level.

I am a spiritual risk taker. Often when I embark on my next risk, a deeper layer of fears from my ego mind rise up. Initially, my nervous system wants to freeze and shut down because that is familiar. Even though my soul wants to guide me to trust and surrender to Spirit, I often encounter that fear of being exposed. I felt this fear the night before recording my interview for my first Healing Trauma through Conscious Embodiment Summit. I lay in

266

bed with frozen eyes, a thumping heart, and racing thoughts of worry that I would not find the right words and would end up humiliating myself in front of thousands of people.

Thankfully, my soul guided me to start a breathwork session in bed. It only took a few minutes before I started gagging and then ran to my bathroom and hovered over my toilet, purging the energetic anxiety from my solar plexus and sacrum. This process is managing fear by clearing my energy so I can sleep and then be able to take my next step. But what I was about to experience with Grandmother, was a much deeper healing of my wound.

Purging and reclaiming

I reached in front of me for the bucket that was given to each of us at the beginning of the ceremony. I was being called to surrender deeply without any guarantee of where this process was taking me. I saw spirits welcoming me into the bucket. "It is your role to hold people's hand as they dive into their darkness." I surrendered and let go completely. It was as though my body dissolved into the space around me.

This act of purging emanated from my sacrum, and the pain was excruciating. It was like each dry heave originated in my pelvis and shot upwards through my throat. But nothing was coming out of me except air. Suddenly, what felt like a little chunk of something dislodged and flew into the plastic bucket. I collapsed back into the bamboo wall, depleted and weightless.

Then I heard this incredible lullaby floating into my energy field. It sounded like the Divine Mother was singing softly into my ears as she held and rocked me, soothing all of the humiliation from my inner child. My breathing became soft, and I sunk into this soothing support. The shaman sounded like she was singing just for me. Was that possible?

I later found out that what she was singing was called an *icaro*. Icaros are traditional indigenous Amazonian songs that the healers sing during the ceremony to rebalance the patient's body and release negative blockages. These icaros are songs of pure light, inducing divine, blissful feelings in participants while performing deep energetic reparations.

Finally grounded and at peace

It was then that my body became flushed and saturated with this enormous glow. Everywhere I looked, there was love pouring through this misty lens. The amount of unconditional love, forgiveness, and joy that I was experiencing was a hundred-fold more than I could ever imagine feeling in my body and it overtook my mind. I was no longer managing my fear, it was being healed.

Then just like in the sweat lodge, I heard the voice of the shaman in the darkness calling to me, "Gregorio, sing." I replied, "What?" I froze again. What could I sing that would be meaningful for this sacred ceremony? She replied, "Just sing." So, I closed my eyes, took a deep breath, and surrendered to the light within me that resided deep in my heart. I opened my mouth and trusted the tones that flowed out of me, which created this angelic, etheric, and soothing melody that I could never have created on my own. I was connected to this beautiful flow of energy cascading through me that I shared with every soul and spirit in that little bamboo house and beyond.

Later, I was told that my voice grounded the ceremony, which was needed at that time. Again, I was guided and trusted to lead and provide healing for a ceremony that I wasn't at all familiar with, yet I was. I had sung those tones before, just not in this lifetime. The shaman later told me that I was a pillar of light, with light emanating from my hands, and that she had relied on me to give strength during the ceremony.

Awakened and transformed

When I approached the altar for my last cup of tea, the shaman said that my second chakra opened. The medicine helped my purge. The release had opened a channel of energy flow in my body that had been shut down since I was a very young boy. When my second chakra opened, I felt my blood flow into my pelvis in ways I had never experienced before. Instead of feeling contracted, I began to sense my power and creative energy in this area where so much shame and shrinking had resided for so long.

When I returned home, I met one of my former teachers and she reflected how joyful she was that I seemed so empowered. She always knew I held wisdom, but struggled to pull it out of me because I was so shut down. Another friend told me, "Gregg, your transformation is phenomenal. I can sense it, see it, and feel it. It's like you have dropped so deeply into yourself that you flow from a place of personal authority and exude such foundational depth. If I had not just witnessed your transformation, I would not believe it was possible. My jaw is still dropped at the shift in you."

I could feel the shift as well. The purpose of my sacred journey had been revealed. I am not only a healer, but I am a leader. Looking back on my experience, it takes so much courage to surrender, trust, and let go in the healing process when you often do not know where the process will take you. When we can welcome

269

our contractions, breathe into them, and express and release our feelings fully, we always encounter an even deeper experience of the vibration of love on the other side of our pain. And we reclaim our innocence.

I will always remember the shame I felt in that first circle in kindergarten. Having transformed, I now honor that memory with compassion as I enter new circles with the purpose of healing others, acting as a bridge between the non-ordinary and ordinary worlds and being an embodied leader in service to this world.

About The Author

Gregg Westwood MA is a spiritual risk-taker. He is a creative embodied healer, coach, author, consultant, teacher, and leader of transformational experiences. Committed to manifesting the most authentic expression of his soul on this planet, he supports others in discovering their soul's unique creative expression. He assists others in releasing their physical, mental and emotional blocks, fears and challenges, and supports them in reconnecting with their inner joy, embodying their true self and living in vibrant health.

A former professional dancer, actor, massage therapist, and somatic psychotherapist, he honors the wisdom of the body and the healing power of creative expression. Gregg's healing practice is called *Depth Integration* and he works with private clients worldwide. He is the host of the Healing Trauma through Conscious Embodiment and the Conscious Embodiment Summits, an author in the book *Dare to Dream*, and the creator of online and in-person workshops and retreats.

Connect with Gregg online: depthintegration.com

271

Marijuana, I Apologize
Love, Sandra Dee

The year is 2023. I am currently 60 years old.

I've never been married and never had kids and oh yeah…I've been a criminal for over 40 years.

40 years of denial and hiding from the law helped to put my self-esteem in the dirt.

My life was a secret…and it was a shitshow. It was a secret shitshow. (Try saying THAT five times!)

This secret shitshow is what CAUSED me to become and REMAIN a lawbreaker until 2018 when I left North Carolina and returned to Los Angeles, California, "The City of Angels. " That is where I had previously worked as a full-time freelance artist for 15 glorious years.

When I crossed the state lines back into California, I was no longer a criminal. The rules had changed. Marijuana was finally legal…there. For the first time in over 40 years, I was NOT a criminal!

I first used marijuana when I was 14 years old. I was introduced to it by my best friend's mother, in the privacy and safety of their home. I was there for sleepovers and their German mother was a blonde, blue-eyed hipster who kept a beautiful home, cooked wonderful food, and liked Rock and Roll music. Unlike MY mother, she was always happy.

She also smoked weed with her three daughters and allowed them to invite their friends over to do the same if they wished.

Her philosophy was basically, "Stay home where it's safe. Your friends can come over and you don't have to be on the streets." It was always a wonderful time...till my "Killjoy" mother heard what was going on one day and angrily picked me up from my friend's house unannounced. Oh, my mother was on fire. She hated drugs and alcohol, and she was absolutely outraged at what was going on. I was not allowed to go back there ever again.

Where there's a will, there's a way and of course, I found a way because I liked being there. I knew we would smoke, and I would feel better instantly. I would feel peaceful, content, and creative. The desire to die would vanish. Life would become good for the time I was there.

My mother was a Korean war survivor with PTSD. She was barely able to speak English and had two daughters and one "mentally disabled" son. Her husband was in the United States Army and always serving overseas in Vietnam. I have no memory of ever being with my father in person until I was in the third grade. Until I was eight years old, my father was a black and white photo in a 4"x6" picture frame that I would kiss when my mother faithfully showed it to me every night before I went to sleep.

My father was a white American but the rest of us looked Asian. We were the target of merciless racial slurs and bullying almost every time we left our house in North Carolina. Many times, my "special needs" little brother endured physical assaults at school. He would come home bruised and/or scratched but unable to tell us what had happened or who had been involved. It was heartbreaking. No one helped.

My mother struggled to learn English and she worked two factory jobs at night and on the weekends. I was often left in charge of my little brother and sister, and I sometimes jokingly say that I was the mother of two children at the age of six. Life was tough and it seemed to just keep getting tougher. I had inherited my mother's war trauma in utero. So, my sensitivities were already heightened before I was even born, and they only increased as life happened.

My first memory of depression was when I was six. That's when I started first grade in the United States. I experienced school and the general public for the first time, and it was not good.

My suicidal ideation began when I was ten and in the fifth grade. To my sad recollection, the school was more like a prison yard. The kids were punks, and the teachers were angry, sadistic prison guards. Their goal was survival, and they simply had no time or interest in mollycoddling a sensitive minority child enrolled in their public school system. I guess they had tenure. They were useless from MY perspective. Dead weight.

The punks were allowed to bully me and my little brother and sister every day without reprimand. We were regularly mocked, imitated, laughed at, and called names like "Chink," "Retard," "Gook," "Jap," "Kung Fu," "Dog eater," "Prostitute," etc., day after day, year after year.

No one ever helped. Not a fellow student. Not a teacher. Not a principal. Not a parent. No one. I learned early on that I was on my own and there were a lot of rude, vicious people in public. My poor mother was angry, depressed, and tired all the time.

There was rarely any joy to be found inside or outside of my house. I cried myself to sleep every night. I fantasized about ways to end my life. Quietly. Discreetly. And as neatly as possible.

Some kids fantasized about going to Disneyland. I fantasized about lying in a coffin. No sense of pride. No self-esteem. No will to live.

Drugs and alcohol

Throughout my life, I have only seen pot smokers portrayed on TV and in films as low-functioning dimwits for the most part. Shown only to make people laugh at how "stoned and stupid" the pot smokers look.

Meanwhile, alcohol...

I have an unpopular opinion about alcohol. I do not like it. I am perplexed about why it's even legal and why public "bars" are even a thing. How does it make sense that this poison called "alcohol", which is known to be physically addictive and deadly in a variety of ways, is accepted in ANY society?

I've researched alcohol, marijuana, cocaine, heroin, and opiate pain pills. Alcohol is in a league all its own... potentially more destructive than any "drug".

Marijuana is practically benign when compared to the aforementioned substances. In its organic form, marijuana is NOT physically addictive, and no one has ever died from smoking too much of it.

If you consume an alcoholic beverage every day, you are either already addicted...or you are becoming addicted. In other words, if you drink every day, you are either already an alcoholic or you are becoming one. I have found that some people get extremely worked up about this assertion. At the end of the day, however, it is just a scientific fact.

Furthermore, in certain cases, if a person tried to quit drinking suddenly ("cold turkey"), they could die. Habitual alcohol use as well as its abrupt, medically unsupervised cessation has killed people.

If a habitual user of marijuana suddenly stopped, they might experience temporary irritability or they might not...but no physical withdrawal symptoms occur and certainly not death. I know this from personal experience. There have been several times in my life when I made the decision to stop using it, and I never once had physical withdrawals.

I stopped when I thought I might be drug tested for employment. I stopped when I thought my mother might be right – that I could be destroying my brain. I stopped when I went through periods where it was just too difficult or demeaning to chase the illegal substance down. I stopped when I just wanted to prove to myself that I COULD. And I DID.

I realize some would argue that marijuana is psychologically addictive, and I would not disagree. MANY things are psychologically addictive including food, sex, playing video games, and TikTok.

In a perfect world, none of us would be addicted to anything. But trauma exists. And trauma is often the root cause of physical or mental addiction. To be clear, addiction of any form should be examined and assessed and there is definitely a spectrum of "harm level versus benefit" for whatever we might use to make ourselves feel better. Usually, legality dictates acceptability.

My mother angrily and regularly assured me that people who smoked marijuana were killing their brain cells. They were criminals and not to be trusted. They were lawbreakers with no regard for authority. And they were unwelcome in her house. That included me. If she ever found out I was smoking weed, she would call the police herself and have me arrested. I could never tell my mother the truth.

My secret medicine

Marijuana quelled the rage that bubbled inside me. It made me stop hating people. It allowed me to focus on everything that was GOOD in my life. It reminded me that I had food and shelter and parents who did not use drugs or drink alcohol or molest or beat us. Yes, my life was a shitshow, but weed always reminded me of the good things in my world.

This was my medicine but every time I had to chase it, it chipped away at my self-esteem because I was breaking the law. Tearing myself down became a habit, and I would tear "Maryjane" down as well.

I hid my habit from parents, teachers, fellow students, and friends as well as doctors and employers. It was exhausting. It was the one lie that was always present in my life.

Not only did I have to pretend that I didn't USE marijuana, but I also had to pretend that I was AGAINST it. God. What a betrayal to myself AND to this life-saving herb.

Now don't get me wrong. Weed is not for everyone. Lots of things are not for everyone.

The way I have consumed my plant medicine is through smoking it. Even though I have always tried to implement a water filtration device (known as a "bong" or "bubbler"), I know that smoking is smoking. Smoking in ANY form is NOT an "optimal" thing to do to one's body, BUT for me the healing effects of smoking marijuana far outweigh any downside.

However, as I mentioned, society likes to beat the drum of whatever beliefs they have been indoctrinated with, and still to this day in the year 2023, there are people who drink alcohol while they bemoan the perils of "legalizing marijuana". They just don't know what they just don't know.

I am STILL not completely comfortable talking about it, but for me to continue to keep this a secret only perpetuates the circle of shame and blame in my life. Society beat me down early on and made me feel bad…and then it made me feel worse. I had no coping skills when I first started self-medicating. Marijuana got me through some terrible times, but the shadow of secrecy was heavy, and I always questioned the validity of the bad rap it seemed to get on the "TV NEWS" programs. Maybe they were right?

There was a time when if ANYthing went wrong in my life, I blamed it on my "drug use". I blamed marijuana for the water heater springing a leak! I blamed marijuana for a flat tire!

I did this for decades. But today? Today, I can tell you this: LIFE is a F.O.R.D. – "Fix or repair daily."

I found this to be true whether I was (or am) using marijuana or not. Life is just a series of ups and downs, and each new day presents opportunities to practice "creative problem solving."

Life is ugly and life is beautiful, sometimes on the very same day.

I was wrong to have ever blamed marijuana for anything.

Marijuana brought me PEACE and HEALING. It was (is) my medicine. To me, using marijuana has NOTHING to do with "partying" and having a "good time". I do not nor have I ever considered myself to be a "party person." What I have ALWAYS been is a "seeker of peace and understanding."

Marijuana is NOT the "enemy." IGNORANCE is the enemy. Ignorance is always the enemy.

I owe her an apology

Dear Marijuana, I'm sorry for all the lies I believed about you. I'm sorry for denying that I knew you. I'm sorry that I didn't talk about you to other people who might have benefited from your healing power the way I did.

I'm sorry for hiding you.

All you have ever done is make me feel better...make life livable...even enjoyable. You have brought me peace while I did the hard work of living. You brought me contentment and clarity surrounding the truth of my life and my future. You gave me a future. Thank you for that.

If and when the time comes for us to part ways, it will be because YOU have helped get me to the place where I COULD even think about saying goodbye to you. But you are like any other relationship or connection in this world...here for a reason, season, or a lifetime. Heck, maybe you're here for ALL of it.

I know you. I vouch for you. You are a healer. You are life-saving medicine in many ways. How could I ever forget the dark nights of the soul you have gotten me through?

I will never forget how it was YOU that got me through the chemotherapy and radiation treatments when I was diagnosed with breast cancer. I was able to live through the shitshow that was my former life because of you, Maryjane. When PTSD gripped me by the throat and tried to kill me, it was you that protected me. You saved me.

You have been known by a variety of names. We've called you Maryjane, weed, grass, ganja, herb, chronic, cannabis... but a rose called by any other name smells just as sweet ... and a marijuana flower called by any other name is just as healing.

I am sorry that you have been so misunderstood. You have been shrouded in so many lies but the truth is, you are beautiful and you are NEEDED in this traumatized world. You deserve to be recognized. Today, I acknowledge you and all you've done for me and undoubtedly, countless others.

I wish I could have expressed this truth before. But I am speaking my truth now and I ask that you forgive me, and I already know that you will, that you already have…because you are a peacemaker. You bring peace and salvation.

Maryjane, thank you for saving my life.

About The Author

Sandra Dee has devoted her entire adult life to understanding herself and the world.

She produced and hosted "LIVE" standup comedy in Los Angeles in 2007 in her attempt to "create and enjoy laughter". It was an eye-opening experience.

She studied art and psychology at Fayetteville State University and describes herself as a lifelong learner. She is also freakishly sensitive and would appreciate it if you wouldn't look at her in the wrong tone of face…especially if she doesn't understand the assignment and it involves a computer.

Sandra Dee has maintained a career as a professional freelance illustrator and muralist for many affluent celebrity clients since 1984. Her artwork was featured on "Oprah" when she first moved to Los Angeles in 1995 after painting a mural for Holly Robinson-Peete. She gained a steady flow of customers in California as well as North Carolina.

Admittedly, she's an introvert with enough acting skills to be extroverted when the situation calls for it, but her preference is always quiet solitude. Her favorite thing about herself is her vivid imagination. She has never been bored a single moment of her life.

Sandra Dee, still a freelance artist, is happily single and is the doting mother to three beautiful rescue chihuahuas, Rocky, Coco, and June, and…she is no longer a criminal.

Life is good.

Connect with Sandra Dee and her art at www.theartofsandradee.com

Marijuana / Santa Maria

Marijuana, also known as cannabis, has been used for centuries for its medicinal properties, particularly in traditional indigenous practices. One specific strain of marijuana that has gained popularity in recent years for its healing properties is Santa Maria.

Santa Maria is a sativa-dominant strain of marijuana that is known for its uplifting and energizing effects. It is often used for its medicinal properties, such as pain relief, mood enhancement, and stress reduction. Some users also report that Santa Maria can help with creative inspiration and focus, making it a popular choice among artists and writers.

In addition to its physical and mental health benefits, Santa Maria is also sometimes used for spiritual and ceremonial purposes. Some spiritual communities believe that the use of marijuana can help to facilitate spiritual experiences and enhance one's connection to the divine.

It is important to note that the use of marijuana, including Santa Maria, can have potential risks and side effects, especially if used excessively or without proper guidance. Some of the reported risks associated with marijuana use include cognitive impairment, respiratory problems, and the potential for addiction or dependency.

Additionally, while the use of marijuana is legal for medicinal or recreational purposes in some countries or states, it is still illegal in many parts of the world, and possession or distribution of the drug can result in serious legal consequences. As with any substance, it is important to approach the use of marijuana, including Santa Maria, with caution and responsibility.

Conclusion

As we come to the end of our Psychedelic Hero's Journey, we are left with a deep sense of awe and wonder at the transformative power of sacred plant medicine. Through the stories shared in this book, we have seen how these medicines have the ability to awaken our innermost selves, help us face our fears, and open us up to profound spiritual experiences. The contributors to this book have generously shared their personal experiences with these sacred medicines and shamanic ceremonies, offering us a glimpse into the potential for healing, growth, and spiritual awakening that they hold.

We hope that this book has provided you with insight, inspiration, and perhaps even guidance on your own journey of self-discovery and spiritual awakening. Let us also remember that the journey of self-discovery and spiritual awakening is ongoing. The experiences shared in this book are but a snapshot of a much larger tapestry of human experience. Let us continue to learn from each other, to seek out new perspectives and insights, and to cultivate a deeper understanding of ourselves and the world around us.

May we also remember to approach the use of sacred plant medicine with reverence, respect, and caution, and to seek out experienced and trustworthy guides who can help us navigate these powerful experiences safely and responsibly. Let us honor the traditions and cultures that have developed around these medicines and work to preserve and protect them for future generations.

Above all, may we never forget that the most important journey is the one we take within ourselves. May we continue to cultivate love, compassion, and understanding for ourselves and others, and may we always strive to be the hero of our own story, emboldened by the transformative power of sacred medicine and the wisdom of the ages.

Appendix

To support you in your exploration, education and experiential journeys with psychedelics and shamanic rituals, I've provided you with some information on how to prepare for, integrate and journal about your sessions.

Preparation

Psychedelic journeys and shamanic rituals are becoming increasingly popular as people seek alternative methods for healing and spiritual exploration. However, these experiences can be intense and potentially challenging, which is why it's important to prepare both physically and mentally beforehand. Here are some of the best ways to prepare for a psychedelic journey or shamanic ritual.

Self-Care

Self-care is essential when preparing for a psychedelic journey or shamanic ritual. This includes getting plenty of rest and sleep, staying hydrated, and avoiding alcohol and drugs in the days leading up to the experience. It's also important to create a safe and comfortable environment for the journey or ritual, with things like comfortable seating, blankets, and pillows.

Nutrition

Nutrition is also an important factor to consider when preparing for a psychedelic journey or shamanic ritual. It's best to avoid heavy, greasy, or processed foods in the days leading up to the experience, as these can make you feel sluggish and uncomfortable. Instead, focus on eating fresh fruits and vegetables, plant protein, and whole grains. It's also a good idea to avoid caffeine and sugary drinks, as these can make you feel jittery and anxious.

Meditation

Meditation can be a powerful tool for preparing for a psychedelic journey or shamanic ritual. It can help you calm your mind, reduce anxiety, and connect with your inner self. Try to establish a daily meditation practice in the weeks leading up to the experience, even if it's just for a few minutes each day. Spend time in quiet contemplation to help calm your mind and reduce any anxiety or fear you may be feeling. You can also try guided meditations that focus on relaxation, visualization, and spiritual connection. There are several guided meditations you can listen to or download at SacredMedicineStories.com.

Psychotherapy

Psychotherapy can be a valuable tool for anyone considering a psychedelic journey or shamanic ritual. A therapist can help you explore any underlying issues or traumas that may be impacting your life, and work through them in a safe and supportive environment. They can also help you integrate any insights or revelations from the experience into your daily life.

Shadow Work

Shadow work is the process of exploring and integrating the darker aspects of your psyche. It can be challenging but ultimately rewarding work, and it's especially important when preparing for a psychedelic journey or shamanic ritual. The experience can bring up unresolved emotions, fears, and traumas, and shadow work can help you navigate these difficult feelings in a healthy and productive way. Shadow work can involve therapy, journaling, and other forms of self-exploration. Check out Dr. 1Drea's free course excerpt, *"Psychedelic Shadow Work: Illuminating and Integrating the Dark Side for Healing and Transformation"* at SacredMedicineStoires.com.

Community Support

Finally, it's important to have a support system in place when preparing for a psychedelic journey or shamanic ritual. This can include friends, family, or a trusted spiritual community. It's important to have someone to talk to before and after the experience, and to feel supported throughout the journey or ritual.

Journaling

Journaling is another effective way to prepare for a psychedelic journey or shamanic ritual. Writing down your thoughts, feelings, and intentions can help you clarify your goals for the experience and work through any fears or anxieties you may have. You can also use your journal to reflect on the experience afterward and integrate any insights or revelations into your daily life.

Here are 15 journal prompts that can be helpful with preparing for psychedelic journeys and shamanic ceremonies:

1. What fears or anxieties do I have about this experience? Why do I think I feel this way?
2. What do I hope to gain from this experience? What areas of my life do I hope to explore or heal?
3. What types of past trauma or difficult experiences have I had? How do I think these might impact the experience?
4. What aspects of myself or my life do I feel disconnected from or have trouble accessing? Why do I think this is the case?

288

5. What emotions or feelings do I tend to avoid or suppress? How do I think this might come up during the experience?

6. What types of shadows or negative patterns do I recognize in myself? How have these impacted my life in the past?

7. What types of positive qualities or strengths do I possess that I want to focus on during the experience?

8. What relationships in my life are most important to me? How might these come up during the experience?

9. How do I feel about my body and physical sensations? How might these be impacted during the experience?

10. What are my beliefs or attitudes about spirituality or the universe? How might these impact my experience?

11. What types of self-care practices do I find most helpful for reducing anxiety or stress? How can I incorporate these into my preparation routine?

12. What types of support do I have in my life (friends, family, therapist, etc.)? How can I ensure I feel supported during and after the experience?

13. What types of art, music, or other creative activities do I find most inspiring or meaningful? How can I incorporate these into my preparation routine?

14. What types of activities or experiences make me feel most grounded or connected to my true self? How can I incorporate these into my preparation routine?

15. What lessons or insights have I gained from previous psychedelic or shamanic experiences? How can I apply these to my preparation for the current experience?

In conclusion, preparing for a psychedelic journey or shamanic ritual requires a holistic approach that addresses physical, mental, and spiritual aspects of your life. By taking care of your body, mind, and soul, you can set the stage for a transformative and healing experience. Remember, it's not just about the journey itself, but also the integration of the experience into your daily life afterward.

Integration

Integrating psychedelic experiences into everyday life can be challenging, as the profound nature of these experiences can make it difficult to return to "normal" life. Integration is a crucial aspect of working with psychedelics and shamanic ceremonies because it allows individuals to make sense of and apply the insights and experiences gained during the experience to their everyday lives.

Psychedelic experiences and shamanic ceremonies can often provide profound insights into one's psyche, relationships, life purpose, and spirituality. However, if these insights are not integrated properly, they may fade over time or remain elusive and difficult to understand. Integration is the process of making sense of these insights and applying them to one's everyday life. It is the bridge between the insights gained during the experience and the lasting positive changes in one's life.

Integration involves reflection, self-care, and the development of new habits and practices that support one's goals and values. It can include journaling, therapy, meditation, creative expression, physical exercise, and other activities that help individuals process and integrate their experiences.

Without proper integration, individuals may experience a range of challenges, including difficulty making sense of the experience, feeling overwhelmed or confused, or failing to apply the insights gained to their everyday lives. Integration can also help individuals to identify and work through any challenging emotions or experiences that may have arisen during the journey or ceremony, promoting healing and growth.

In summary, integration is important for people taking psychedelics and sitting in shamanic ceremonies because it allows them to make sense of the insights and experiences gained during the experience and apply them to their everyday lives, promoting lasting positive change and growth.

Some ways to integrate these experiences include:

- Reflecting on the experience: Take time to journal or talk to someone about your experience, as this can help you process and integrate the insights you gained.

- Journaling: Journaling can be a powerful tool for reflecting on and integrating insights gained during the psychedelic experience, as well as tracking progress and identifying patterns over time.

- Creative expression: Engaging in creative activities such as painting, writing, or music can help individuals to process and express their insights in a tangible and meaningful way.

- Incorporating insights into daily life: Try to apply any insights or realizations you had during the experience to your daily life, whether it be through changes in your relationships, career, or personal habits.

- Building a supportive community: Seek out others who have had similar experiences and can provide support and understanding. Joining a psychedelic therapy group or psychedelic-assisted therapy program can also be helpful.

- Practicing mindfulness and meditation: Mindfulness practices such as meditation can help you stay present and grounded in the present moment, which can be particularly helpful for integrating the insights gained during a psychedelic experience.

- Therapy: Working with a therapist who is experienced in psychedelic integration can provide a supportive and structured environment for processing and integrating insights, as well as addressing any challenging emotions or experiences that may have arisen during the experience. You may even consider finding a coach who offers integration coaching.

- Lifestyle changes: Making intentional changes to one's lifestyle and habits based on insights gained during the psychedelic experience can be an effective way to integrate those insights into daily life. This might include changes to diet, exercise, social habits, or career goals, among others.

Overall, integration is a deeply personal and ongoing process, and different approaches may work best for different individuals. The important thing is to find practices and strategies that feel meaningful and supportive, and to be patient and compassionate with oneself throughout the integration process.

It's also important to remember that psychedelic experiences, like other experiences, can be challenging and difficult. It's also important to take care of yourself and not to rush the process, and to be open to seeking professional help if needed.

Here are 15 journal prompts that can be helpful for integrating the insights gained during your psychedelic journeys:

1. What were the most significant insights or experiences I had during the psychedelic journey? How did these insights impact me emotionally and intellectually?

2. What parts of myself or my life did I feel more connected to during the journey? How can I cultivate that connection in my daily life?

3. What parts of myself or my life did I feel disconnected from during the journey? How can I work to address that disconnection in my daily life?

4. What types of relationships did I feel most connected to during the journey? How can I deepen those relationships in my daily life?

5. What types of relationships did I feel least connected to during the journey? How can I work to improve those relationships in my daily life?

6. What types of fears or negative patterns did I confront during the journey? How can I work to address those patterns in my daily life?

7. What types of positive qualities or strengths did I recognize in myself during the journey? How can I cultivate those qualities in my daily life?

8. What types of emotions or feelings did I experience during the journey that I typically avoid or suppress in my daily life? How can I work to integrate those emotions in a healthy and productive way?

9. What types of physical sensations did I experience during the journey? How can I use those sensations to deepen my connection with my body in my daily life?

10. What types of creative inspirations or ideas did I have during the journey? How can I use those inspirations or ideas to pursue my passions and goals in my daily life?

11. What types of changes to my daily habits or routines can I make based on the insights gained during the journey? How

can I ensure that those changes are sustainable and meaningful?

12. What types of support do I need in order to integrate the insights gained during the journey? How can I reach out to friends, family, or professionals for that support?

13. What types of challenges or obstacles do I anticipate facing as I integrate the insights gained during the journey? How can I prepare myself to face those challenges in a healthy and productive way?

14. What types of future experiences or opportunities might help me to further integrate the insights gained during the journey? How can I plan for and create those experiences or opportunities?

15. What types of gratitude or appreciation can I cultivate for the insights gained during the journey? How can I express that gratitude in my daily life?

Check out Dr. 1Drea's free integration program, "*Psychedelic Integration & Manifestation: 30 Days of Self-Discovery with Post-Trip Journaling, Meditation & Affirmations*" at SacredMedicineStories.com.

About the Book's Creator

DaeEss 1Drea Pennington Wasio, formerly known as Andrea Pennington, is an integrative physician, acupuncturist, psychedelic assisted therapy facilitator, retreat leader, meditation teacher, creator of The Cornerstone Process for Conscious Evolution and The Attunement Meditation, and international speaker who is on a mission to raise the level of consciousness and real self-love on our planet. She is the proud host of the Conscious Evolution Podcast, founder of the holistic health company, In8Vitality, which integrates ancient wisdom with modern neuroscience and conscious media.

With over two decades of medical practice specialized in trauma recovery, addiction medicine, Traditional Chinese Medicine and acupuncture, for over 20 years Dr. 1Drea has provided medical services, workshops and retreats to help thousands of people build resilience, reclaim vitality after burnout, recover from Adverse Childhood Experiences and nurture real self- love in order to thrive in all areas of life. She is part of the leadership team at Beckley Retreats, where she provides mentorship and ceremony support to a world-class group of facilitators, shamans, and musicians.

As a personal brand architect, media producer, and communications specialist, she leverages her 20+ years of experience in broadcast and digital media to proudly help healers, Light workers and coaches to bring their brilliance to the world through publishing and media production with Make Your Mark Global Media.

Dr. 1Drea is also a bestselling author, international TEDx speaker and documentary filmmaker. For nearly two decades, she has shared her empowering insights on vitality and resilience on The

Oprah Winfrey Show, The Dr. Oz Show, iTV This Morning, CNN, the Today Show, LUXE-TV, Thrive Global and Huffington Post and as a news anchor for Discovery Health Channel. She also produced a four-part documentary series and DVD entitled *Simple Steps to a Balanced Natural Pregnancy.*

Dr. 1Drea has appeared in many print publications including *Essence, Ebony, Newsweek, The Sun, Red, Top Santé,* and *Stylist.* She has also written or contributed to 18 books. As host of the talk show, *Liberate Your Authentic Self* and as founder of In8Vitality, she blends her 'nerdy' mix of medical science, positive psychology, and mindfulness meditation to empower us all to show up authentically, love passionately, and live with vitality.

Visit Dr. 1Drea online at:
1Drea.me
ConsciousEvolution.live
MakeYourMarkGlobal.com
In8Vitality.com

Get Social!
www.facebook.com/DrAndreaPennington
www.twitter.com/drandrea
www.linkedin.com/in/andreapennington
www.instagram.com/daeess.1drea

Other Books Published
by Make Your Mark Global

The Top 10 Traits of Highly Resilient People
Compiled by Daess 1Drea Pennington Wasio, MD

Holistic Healing: 12 real life accounts of healing mind, body and soul by overcoming stress and burnout, processing trauma, rewiring the brain, reprogramming the mind, and integrating the soul
Created & compiled by Daess 1Drea Pennington Wasio, MD

Manifesting Love: Real Life Love Stories of Conscious Relationships Co-created with the Universe
Created & compiled by Daess 1Drea Pennington Wasio, MD

Unity Conscious Leadership™ (Interdependent Growth and Transformation): From a Buddhist Perspective by Dr. Joyce Wazirali

The Real Self Love Handbook: A Proven 5-step Process to Liberate Your Authentic Self, Build Resilience and Live an Epic Life
by Daess 1Drea Pennington Wasio, MD

The Ultimate Self-help Book: How to Be Happy Confident & Stress Free, Change Your Life with Law Of Attraction & Energy Healing by Yvette Taylor

Magic and Miracles
Created and Compiled by Daess 1Drea Pennington Wasio, MD

Life After Trauma
Created and Compiled by Daess 1Drea Pennington Wasio, MD

The Magical Unfolding by Helen Rebello

The Orgasm Prescription for Women
by Daess 1Drea Pennington Wasio, MD

Time to Rise
Created and Compiled by Daess 1Drea Pennington Wasio, MD

The Book on Quantum Leaps for Leaders: The Practical Guide to Becoming a More Efficient and Effective Leader from the Inside Out by Bitta. R. Wiese

Turning Points
Compiled and Edited by Daess 1Drea Pennington Wasio, MD

How to Liberate and Love Your Authentic Self
by Daess 1Drea Pennington Wasio, MD

Daily Compassion Meditation: 21 Guided Meditations, Quotes and Images to Inspire Love, Joy and Peace
by Daess 1Drea Pennington Wasio, MD

Get Published and Share Your Message with the World

Make Your Mark Global is a branding, marketing and media agency based in the USA and the French Riviera. We offer publishing, content development, and promotional services to heart-based, conscious authors who wish to have a lasting impact through the sharing and distribution of their transformative message. We also help authors build a strong online media presence and platform for greater visibility and provide speaker training.

If you'd like help writing, publishing, or promoting your book, or if you'd like to co-author a collaborative book, visit us online or call for a free consultation.

Visit www.MakeYourMarkGlobal.com, or

Call +1 (707) 776-6310 or

Send an email to Booking@AndreaPennington.com